Origami

Origami

BEAUTIFUL OBJECTS FOR YOU TO CREATE STEP BY STEP

Monica Cilmi

To my wonderful son Dylan, the new exciting chapter of my life

This edition published in 2016 by Arcturus Publishing Limited
26/27 Bickels Yard, 151–153 Bermondsey Street,
London SE1 3HA

Copyright © Arcturus Holdings Limited

All rights reserved. No part of this publication may be reproduced, stored in a retrieval system, or transmitted, in any form or by any means, electronic, mechanical, photocopying, recording or otherwise, without prior written permission in accordance with the provisions of the Copyright Act 1956 (as amended). Any person or persons who do any unauthorised act in relation to this publication may be liable to criminal prosecution and civil claims for damages.

ISBN: 978-1-78428-253-0
AD004262UK

Printed in China

CONTENTS

INTRODUCTION 6
MATERIALS 8
GETTING STARTED 10

ANIMALS 14
Butterfly 16
Crane 18
Fish 20
Swan 22
Unicorn 24
Reindeer 26
Peacock or Fantail Crane 28

NATURE 30
Tulip 32
Hydrangea Flower and Leaf 34
Lotus 37
Iris 39
Kusudama Flower 41
Mushroom 43
Rose with Leaf 45

CLASSICS 48
Masu Box 50
Rectangular Box 52
Sweet Container 54
Star Box 56
Tea Plate 58
Heart 60
A Simple Bag 62
Geisha Card 64
Chair 68

CONTEMPORARY 70
Coaster 72
Bowl 74
Spiky Star 76
Standing Plate 78
Hummingbird 80
Contemporary Form 82

KIRIGAMI 84
Fantasy Tree 86
Turtles Decoration 87
Birds 89
Curvy Decoration 90
Cherry Blossom 92
Table Centrepiece 94

STOCKISTS 96

INTRODUCTION

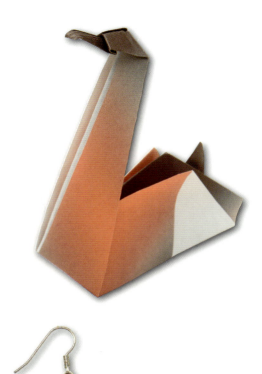

'Origami' is a Japanese word which literally means 'folding paper' – 'ori' means 'fold' and 'kami' means 'paper'. Origami is an ancient art form which still fascinates people and, at its most advanced, can involve high levels of folding expertise that result in splendid, elaborate paper sculptures.

It is amazing how, with just a single sheet of paper and a small number of basic folds, you can produce beautiful and imaginative origami shapes. I am always amazed by the new ideas and designs of origami artists and they inspire me to create my own models.

This book is a guide to the creative world of origami. It includes projects of varying degrees of difficulty, from fairly easy through to hard, and on a wide variety of themes, from nature to modular contemporary. It also contains information about materials, origami bases and folding techniques. For those who want to experiment with paper cutting, there is a section on kirigami later in the book.

I hope exploring these different models will stimulate your imagination and increase your appreciation for the art of origami. With determination and concentration, you'll find you can master this art, but most importantly of all you'll derive great pleasure from the folding process and the results it produces.

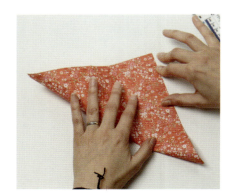

MATERIALS

The main material for origami is paper. There are lots of different types and textures of paper to choose from, including:

- general origami paper (square sheets, coloured on one side or double-sided)
- washi (Japanese handmade paper, ideal for delicate origami models)
- chiyogami (brightly patterned paper)
- aizome (dyed paper)
- shinwazome (raised-pattern paper)
- unryu (dragon paper with swirls on it)

As a beginner, it is useful to start by practising on cartridge paper then progressing to origami paper with one coloured side, which will help you to visualize folding and creases. The other papers are more expensive, but interesting and great to try after you become more practised. The washi paper in particular is ideal for shapes such as the lotus (see page 37) and the geisha card (see page 64). In terms of size, it is advisable to start with paper that is 15cm (6in) square, as this is the most popular medium size; you can progress to larger (and smaller) sizes later on.

Other materials and tools include:

- a notebook, for writing details about diagrams, bases and folding
- pens or pencils, for adding details to certain origami figures
- scissors, occasionally for cutting some origami pieces, but mostly for kirigami
- a gluestick, for attaching smaller parts, such as decorations on boxes
- a ruler, to help create creases and make sure they are clean and sharp

GETTING STARTED

Origami is made from square paper bought from specific shops or online, but ordinary paper cut into a square can be used as well. To make origami models you need to follow diagrams accompanied by specific instructions, symbols and terms. There are some important points to keep in mind when starting to practise origami:

- remember to keep your workspace clean and tidy
- start out using 15cm (6in) square paper as this is the easiest to work with; use origami paper or any thin paper
- practise using ordinary cartridge paper to avoid wasting expensive coloured paper
- when folding, remember always to make sharp creases (a ruler or fingernail can be used)
- if diagrams are difficult to follow, it helps to look ahead at the next illustrations to see how the folded piece should look.

Arrows

On origami diagrams, arrows show you which direction the paper is to be folded in. It is important to understand the different arrow symbols:

- Fold in this direction
- Turn over
- Pleat fold
- Rotate
- Open out
- Insert in this direction

Folds

The two basic origami folds are the valley fold and the mountain fold.

Valley fold
You make a valley fold by folding the bottom edge of the paper up so that the paper forms a 'V' shape.

Mountain fold
A mountain fold is the opposite of a valley fold. You make it by folding the top edge of the paper down so that the paper forms a mountain shape.

Pleat fold
A pleat fold is a valley fold, followed by a mountain fold. A series of pleat folds creates a concertina effect.

Reverse folds

The inside and outside reverse folds are also important. Reverse folds are often used for making the head or tail of an animal. They aren't difficult, but take a bit of practice to get right.

First, fold your square of paper along the diagonal. Then fold the tip along the dotted line, as shown. Fold in both directions so that you get a good crease.

Open the paper slightly and press the tip downwards so that it lies between the two sides of the paper. This is an inside reverse fold.

For an outside reverse fold, crease the tip as before, but this time fold the sides of the paper outwards along the crease.

Press down to complete the outside reverse fold.

Bases

There are several bases commonly used in origami, but we use only two in this book – the bird base and the water-bomb base.

Bird base

1 Fold the square of paper in half, then fold in half again. Open it up.

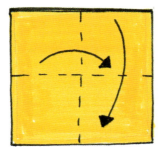

2 Fold the square on the diagonal, both ways

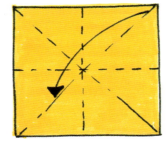

3 The shape will look like this

4 Rotate so that the long, folded side is at the bottom. Reverse-fold the right-hand corner so that it is inside the shape.

5 Now reverse-fold the left-hand corner

6 Your bird base should look like this

Water-bomb base

1 Fold the square of paper in half, then fold in half again. Open it up.

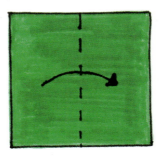

2 Fold the square on the diagonal, both ways

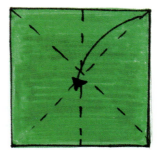

3 Fold in half again. It should look like this.

4 Rotate so that the long, folded side is at the bottom. Reverse-fold the right-hand corner so that it is inside the shape.

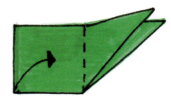

5 Now reverse-fold the left-hand corner

6 Your water-bomb base should look like this

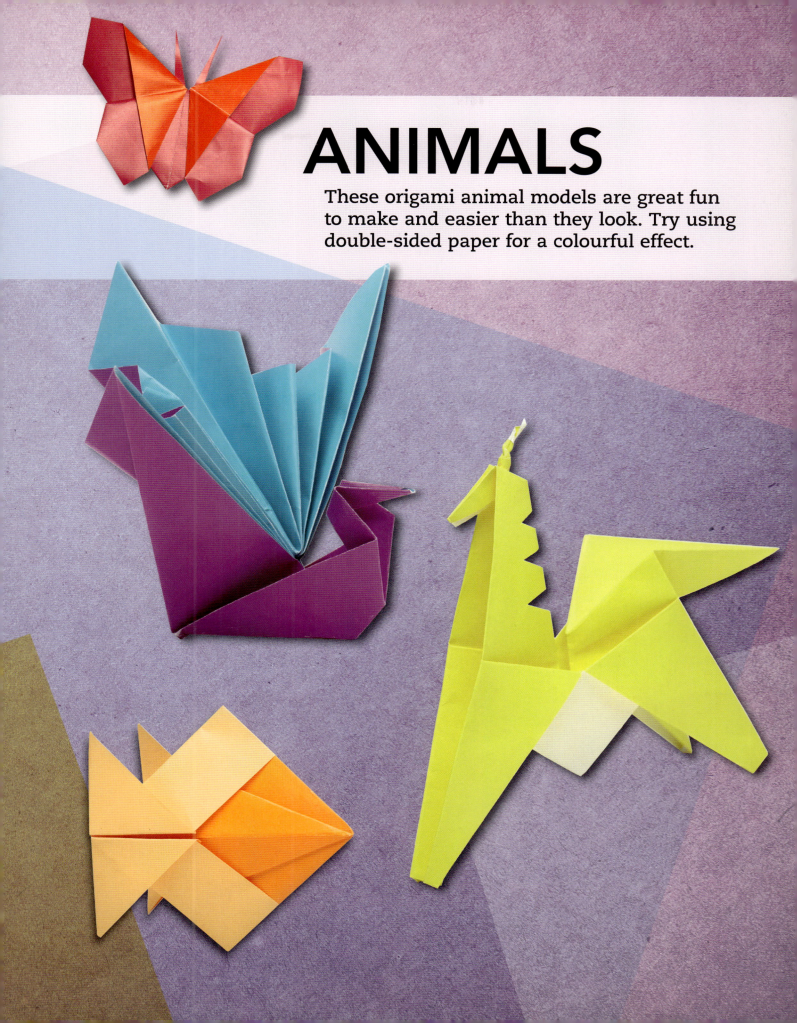

ANIMALS

These origami animal models are great fun to make and easier than they look. Try using double-sided paper for a colourful effect.

BUTTERFLY

This is a fairly easy model to create once you have a bit of know-how. You can make it without the antennae, but I think they add an authentic touch and improve the final look. It is best to use origami paper that is coloured on both sides.

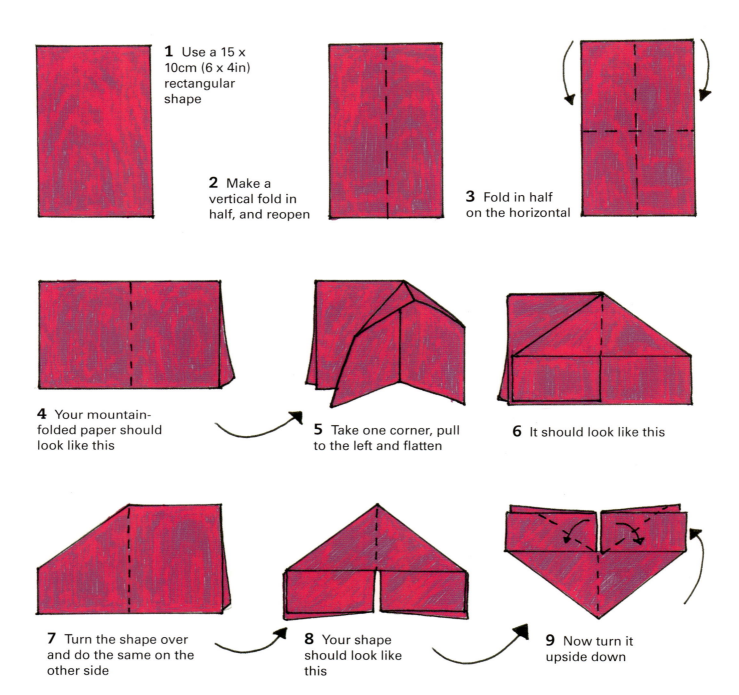

1 Use a 15 x 10cm (6 x 4in) rectangular shape

2 Make a vertical fold in half, and reopen

3 Fold in half on the horizontal

4 Your mountain-folded paper should look like this

5 Take one corner, pull to the left and flatten

6 It should look like this

7 Turn the shape over and do the same on the other side

8 Your shape should look like this

9 Now turn it upside down

medium ★★

10 Fold down the inside edges

11 Fold them up again, noting the creases

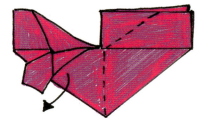

12 Fold along the left crease so that the edge collapses, like this

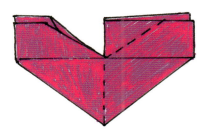

13 Close it to create a valley fold and do the same with the right crease

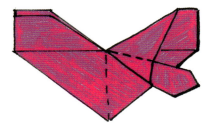

14 Repeat the action, but this time push down the flap

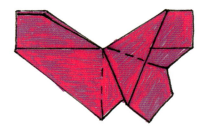

15 Do the same on the other side

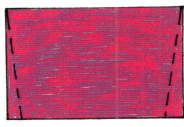

16 Cut two small strips of paper, as shown, for the antennae and attach them separately

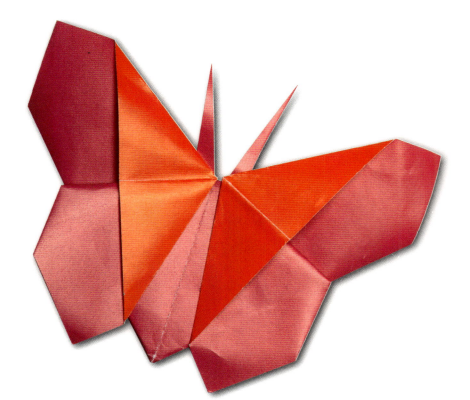

17

CRANE

This is a traditional Japanese model, created from the bird base. It symbolizes peace and longevity and is often used during celebrations. The crane makes a lovely decoration and can be used as either a resting or a flying bird. It is advisable to use thin, coloured origami paper for this model.

1 Using a square of paper 15 x 15cm (6 x 6in), make a bird base

2 Turn it round so that the open end is at the base

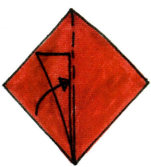

3 Fold the left-hand flap to the centre line

4 Do the same with the right-hand flap

5 Fold down the top point, then open it again

6 Turn over the model and repeat steps 3, 4 and 5 on the other side

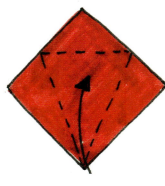

7 Open the flaps and lift up the paper from the bottom corner

8 Press it flat along the creases, as shown

9 Turn the model over and repeat steps 7 and 8 on the other side

10 Fold both flaps to the middle, as shown

11 Turn the model over and do the same on the other side

medium ★★

12 Fold the two bottom flaps up, like this

13 Crease both ways on the diagonal, then inside reverse fold to make the tail

14 Inside reverse fold the other flap to make the neck. Then make a diagonal crease at the point, as shown

15 Make another inside reverse fold to form the head of the crane

16 Fold both wings down and your model is finished

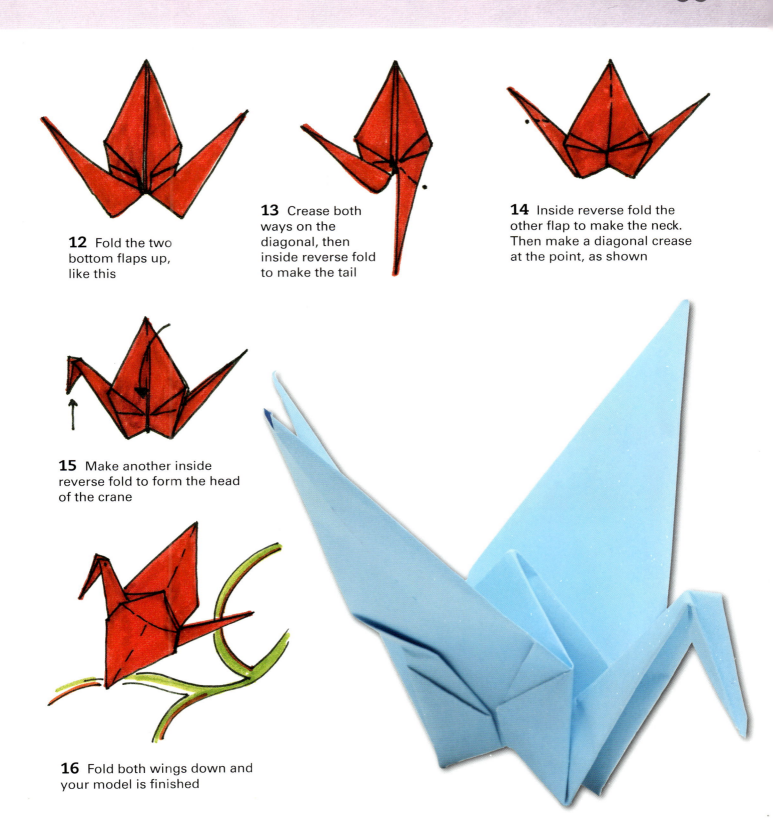

19

FISH

This model is a simple but attractive origami that is often used for good luck. Thanks to its geometric shape, it can be used as a repeat model to create other more abstract objects. The best paper to use is double-sided coloured or patterned origami paper.

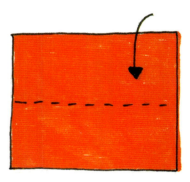

1 Take a piece of paper 15 x 15cm (6 x 6in) square and mountain fold it in half

2 Fold it in half again

3 You should have a square, like this

4 Reopen the paper and fold the corners down along the diagonals, as shown

5 Your shape should look like this

6 Open one flap

7 Put your finger inside the flap

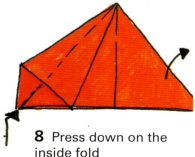

8 Press down on the inside fold

9 Do the same with the other flap

easy ★

10 Fold half of the folding you have just made behind the model; do this on both sides

11 Fold the bottom flap up along the horizontal crease, as shown

12 Do the same on the other side

13 Fold down the small wings; turn the model over

14 Fold down the wings on this side

15 Open the base of the model

16 Press the ends together so that the small flaps meet – this gives you a rhomboid shape

17 You now have your fish – give it eyes for a realistic effect

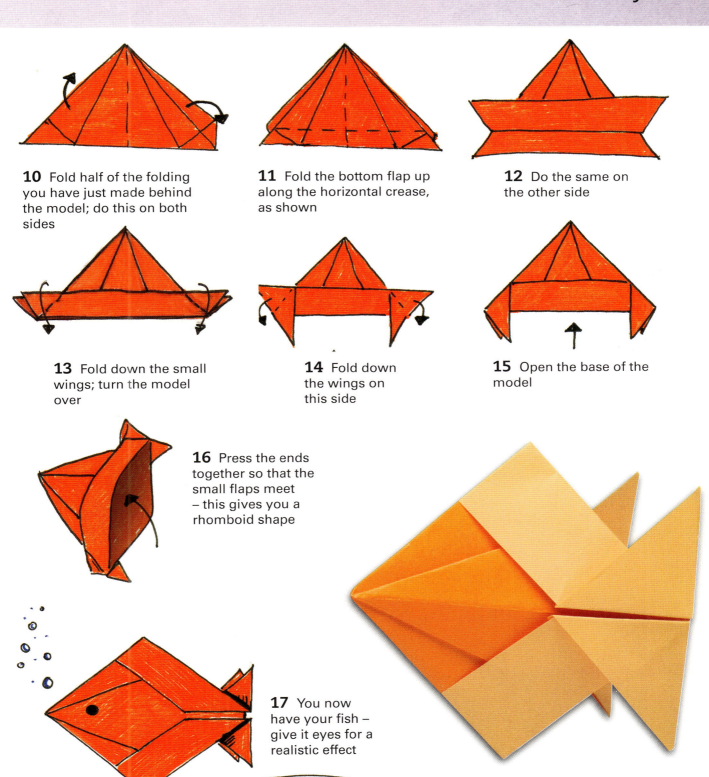

SWAN

The swan is a beautiful and elegant piece, but a bit difficult to make. You need to do various inside reverse folds and some very small folds. It has a kite base and is ideal as a table decoration – it's often used in fancy restaurants and made with napkins. You can use black or white paper if you want to be true to the swan's natural colours, but any coloured paper looks great.

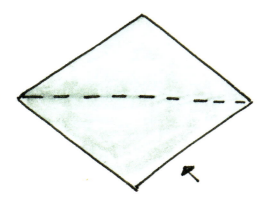

1 Using a square of origami paper, fold in half diagonally to crease, and reopen

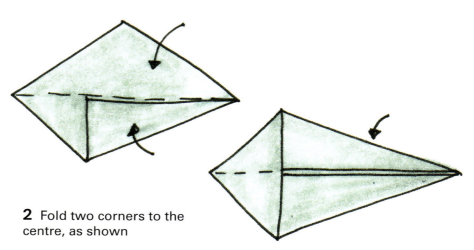

2 Fold two corners to the centre, as shown

3 Fold the shape along the diagonal crease you first made to close it

4 With the model in this position, fold the flap up so that it is level with the top

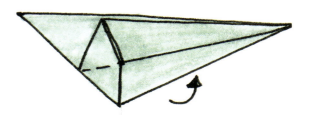

5 Do the same on the other side

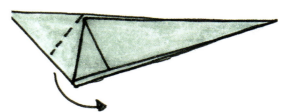

6 Crease along the dotted line both ways and make an inside reverse fold so that the tip is inside the model

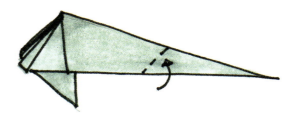

7 Crease along the diagonal line both ways and make an inside reverse fold for the swan's neck

difficult ★★★

8 Crease along the dotted line and make an inside reverse fold to form a small tail

9 Make an inside reverse fold for the head and crease twice on the beak

10 Following the crease lines like an accordion, push in to create the beak

11 Fold the side flap down to make the wing

12 Do the same on the other side

23

UNICORN

This unicorn model can be made using thin or traditional origami paper. It looks great in gold or silver.

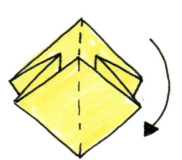

1 Make a bird base

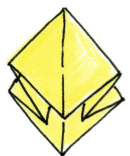

2 Turn it upside down

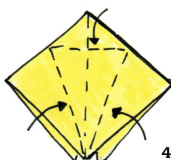

3 Fold to make three creases, as shown

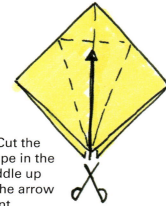

4 Cut the shape in the middle up to the arrow point

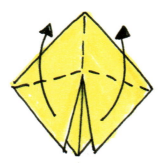

5 Fold up the flaps along the diagonal lines

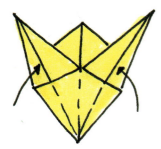

6 Fold the flaps in half to the centre

7 Turn over the model and repeat steps 3–6 on the other side

8 You should now have this shape

9 Turn your model upside down and fold down along the dotted lines, as shown

10 Inside reverse fold the point to make the unicorn's head

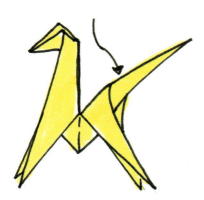

11 Unfold the tail and inside reverse fold it

medium ★★

12 The model should look like this

13 Inside reverse fold at each of the creases shown to make a muzzle and feet

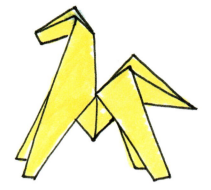

14 Your unicorn should look like this

15 Cut notches for the mane

16 To make a horn, twist a small triangle of paper and attach it inside the head

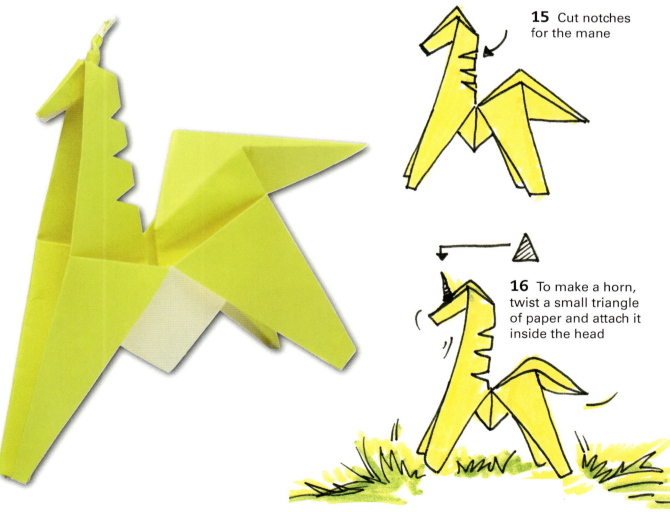

17 Your unicorn is now complete

25

REINDEER

This model is perfect as a Christmas tree decoration. It has a nice shape and is not too hard. There is just one cut to do at the end for the horns. It can be created with any type of traditional origami paper. When you have finished the model, make a small hole in the head and insert a thin string for hanging.

1 Fold a square piece of paper in half along the diagonal and reopen

2 Fold two corners to the centre, along the crease lines shown

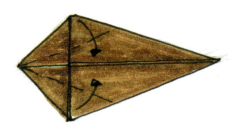

3 Fold again, along the crease lines shown

4 Open up the folds

5 Flatten them . . .

6 . . . so that your model looks like this; then fold it in half

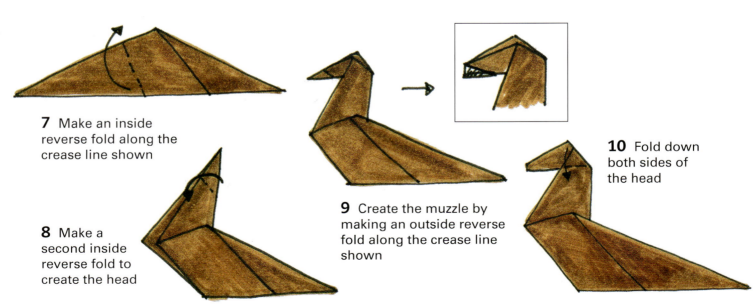

7 Make an inside reverse fold along the crease line shown

8 Make a second inside reverse fold to create the head

9 Create the muzzle by making an outside reverse fold along the crease line shown

10 Fold down both sides of the head

medium ★★

11 For the leg, fold the flap forwards on the crease line shown

12 Then fold it in half backwards on the next crease line. This makes the reindeer's foreleg. Do the same on the other side.

13 To make the hind legs of the reindeer, outside reverse fold along the crease line shown

14 Outside reverse fold the hind legs again

15 At the neck, cut along the dotted line

16 Cut again as shown and fold up to make the ears

17 Your reindeer should now stand proud, like this

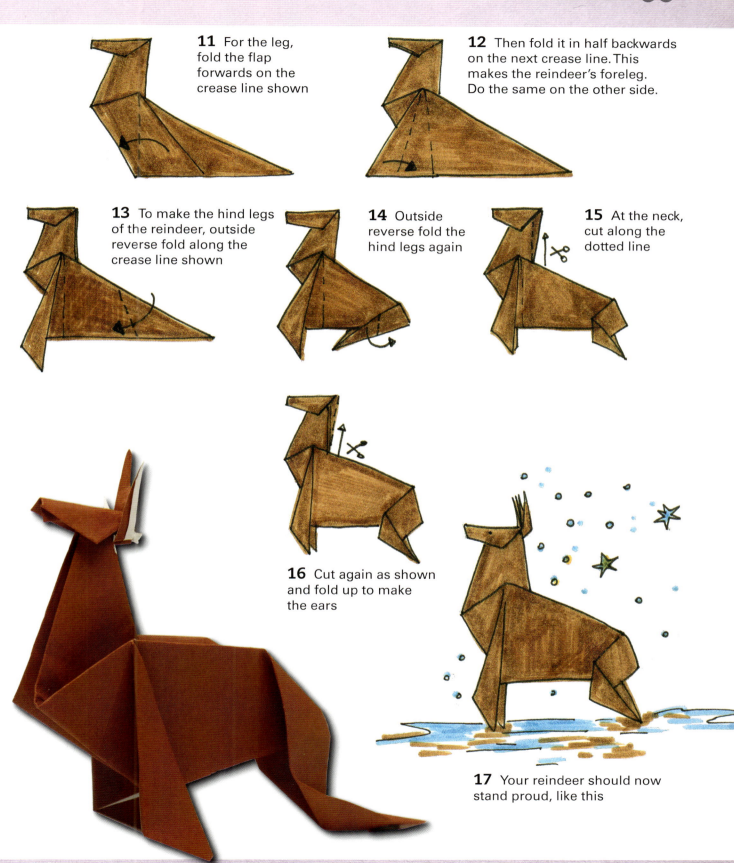

PEACOCK OR FANTAIL CRANE

The peacock is difficult, but very beautiful. It is similar to the crane, but more elaborate. It's best to use double-sided coloured paper to give a nice effect to the inside and outside of the bird's tail.

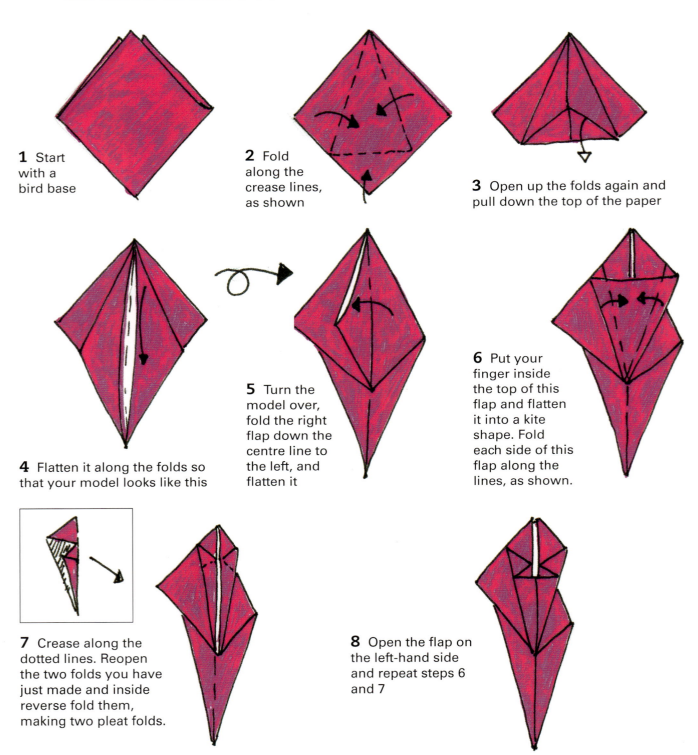

1 Start with a bird base

2 Fold along the crease lines, as shown

3 Open up the folds again and pull down the top of the paper

4 Flatten it along the folds so that your model looks like this

5 Turn the model over, fold the right flap down the centre line to the left, and flatten it

6 Put your finger inside the top of this flap and flatten it into a kite shape. Fold each side of this flap along the lines, as shown.

7 Crease along the dotted lines. Reopen the two folds you have just made and inside reverse fold them, making two pleat folds.

8 Open the flap on the left-hand side and repeat steps 6 and 7

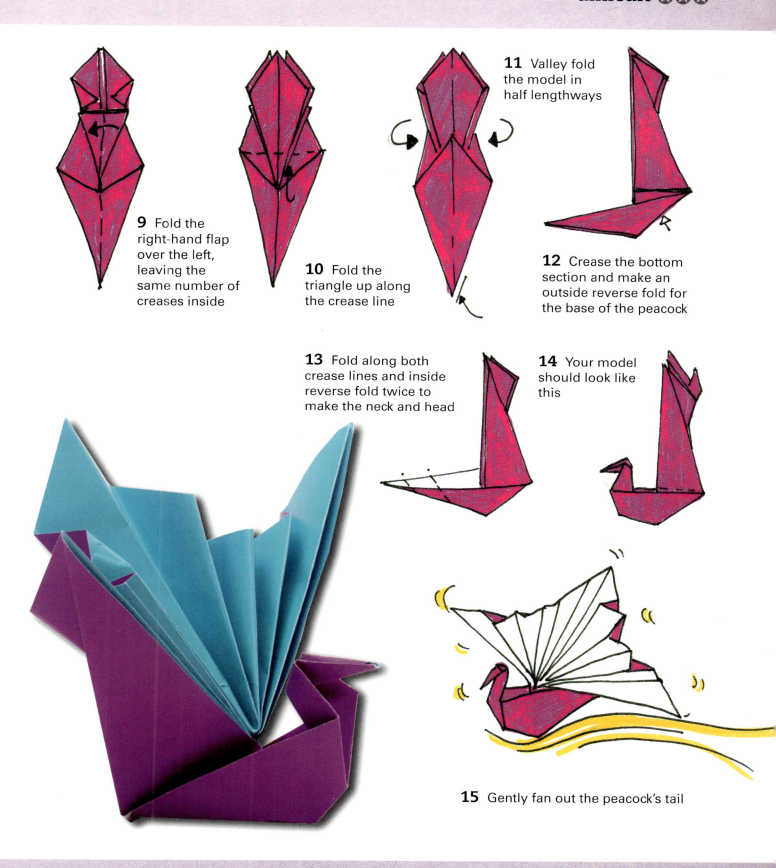

NATURE

You can create wonderful flowers and leaves with origami. Group your nature models together for a beautiful table arrangement.

TULIP

There are two versions of the traditional tulip model. This one is probably the less well-known of the two, but easier to make. It requires two sheets of paper. To create a well-proportioned flower, each sheet has to be a specific size. Here I've used a 15cm (6in) square green sheet of paper for the stem and a 6cm (2½in) square red sheet of paper for the flower. You could also use double-sided or patterned paper for the flower.

STEM

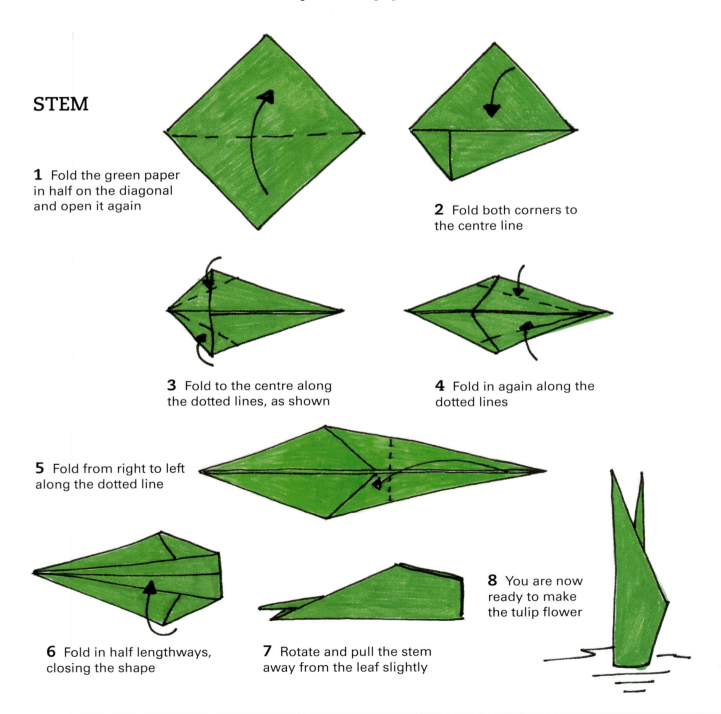

1 Fold the green paper in half on the diagonal and open it again

2 Fold both corners to the centre line

3 Fold to the centre along the dotted lines, as shown

4 Fold in again along the dotted lines

5 Fold from right to left along the dotted line

6 Fold in half lengthways, closing the shape

7 Rotate and pull the stem away from the leaf slightly

8 You are now ready to make the tulip flower

medium ★★

FLOWER

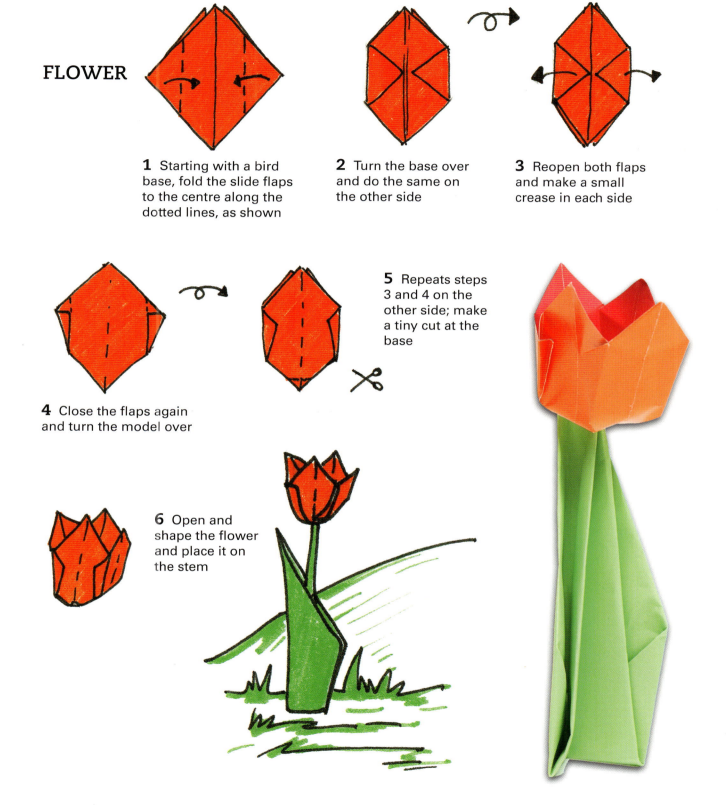

1 Starting with a bird base, fold the slide flaps to the centre along the dotted lines, as shown

2 Turn the base over and do the same on the other side

3 Reopen both flaps and make a small crease in each side

4 Close the flaps again and turn the model over

5 Repeats steps 3 and 4 on the other side; make a tiny cut at the base

6 Open and shape the flower and place it on the stem

HYDRANGEA FLOWER AND LEAF

This model is created small because you need at least five or seven flowers for a composition. Double-sided coloured paper is ideal and the arrangement looks best completed with a leaf.

FLOWER

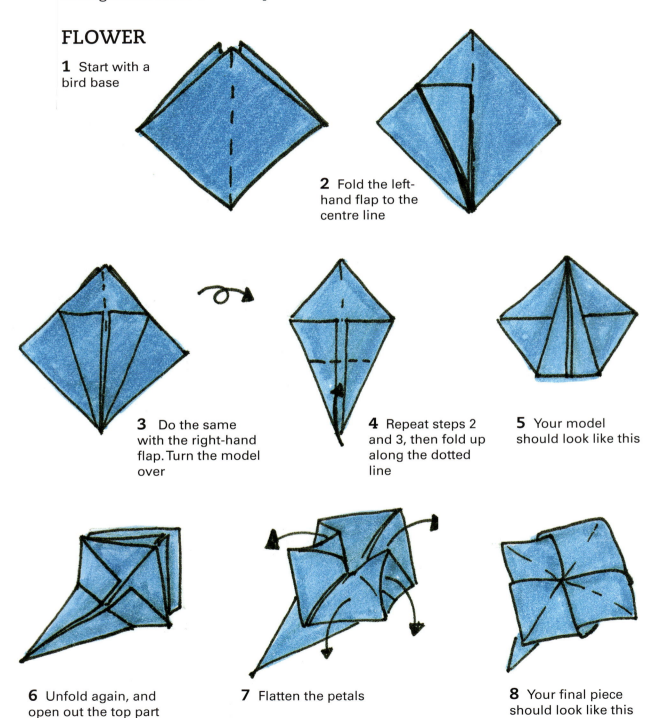

1 Start with a bird base

2 Fold the left-hand flap to the centre line

3 Do the same with the right-hand flap. Turn the model over

4 Repeat steps 2 and 3, then fold up along the dotted line

5 Your model should look like this

6 Unfold again, and open out the top part

7 Flatten the petals

8 Your final piece should look like this

easy ★

9 Add three stamens, cut from a dark piece of paper, to each flower

LEAF

This leaf can be used with the hydrangea and other small flowers, or on its own.

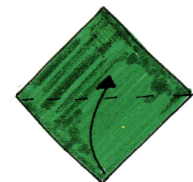

1 Fold a square of paper in half along the diagonal

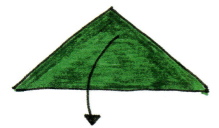

2 Reopen it

3 Fold to the centre along the dotted lines

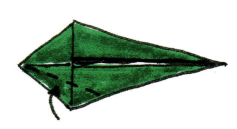

4 Fold in along the dotted line, as shown

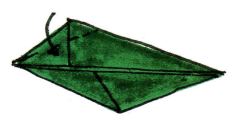

5 Do the same on the opposite side

6 Make a crease along the dotted line and fold down the end

7 Make another, smaller crease and fold up

8 Ensure the point of the folded paper is in line with the centre of the model

9 Valley fold the model in half

10 Rotate, as shown

11 Starting at the left-hand tip, pleat fold the leaf along its length, like an accordion

12 Open out the leaf

13 The flowers and leaf are now ready for your arrangement

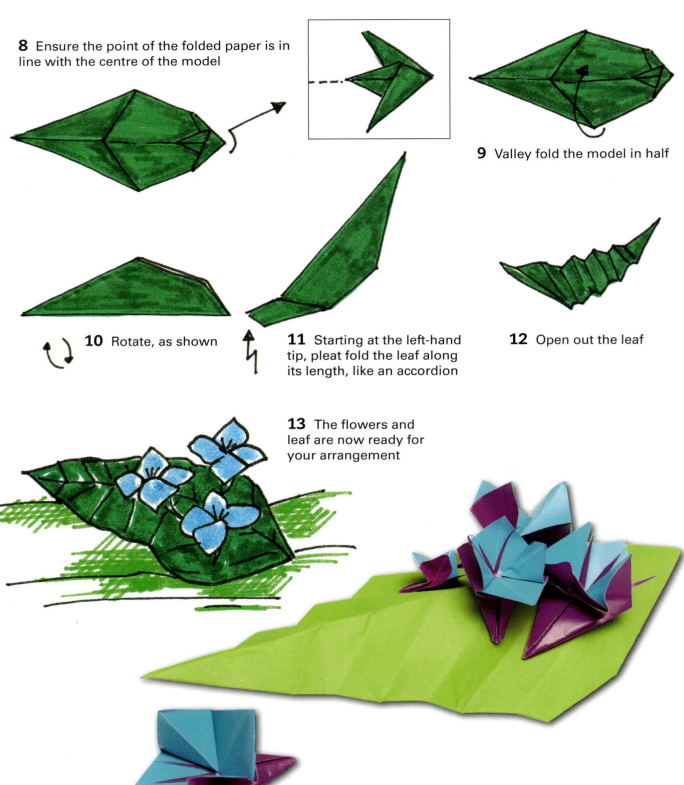

LOTUS

medium ★★

The lotus is the national flower of India and a Buddhist symbol in China and Japan. With this model, the main creases are easy to make, but the final stages can be tricky and the model has to be created with a very flexible, resistant, thin paper. The best is a shiny type of paper sold in outlets such as **The Japanese Shop** (see page 96).

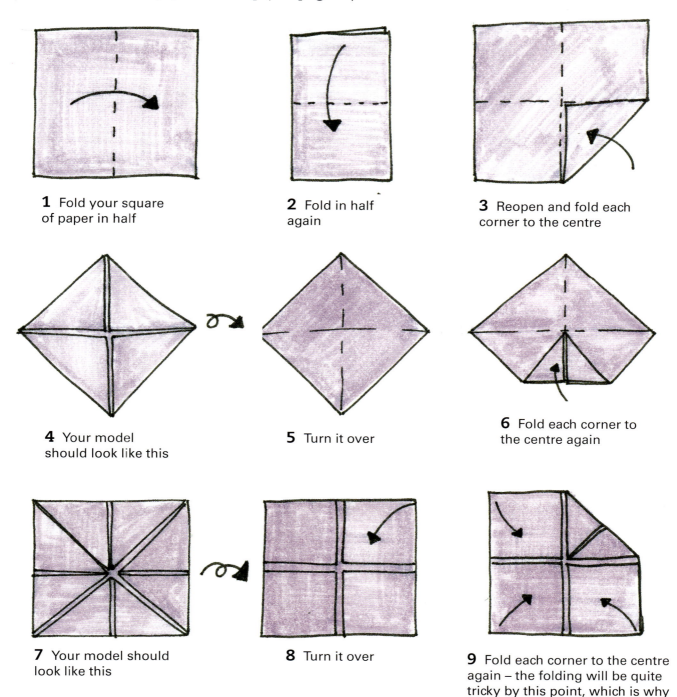

1 Fold your square of paper in half

2 Fold in half again

3 Reopen and fold each corner to the centre

4 Your model should look like this

5 Turn it over

6 Fold each corner to the centre again

7 Your model should look like this

8 Turn it over

9 Fold each corner to the centre again – the folding will be quite tricky by this point, which is why you need to use thin paper

10 Your model should look like this

11 Fold down about a quarter of each corner

12 This gives you the effect of the lotus flower

13 Now lift each of the flaps at the back and bend them so that you create a fuller shape for the petals

14 Your model should look like this

15 Place your finished lotus flower on a leaf. For a more complex model, make four leaves by following the heart model on pages 60–61. Arrange as above and glue them to the bottom of the lotus flower.

38

IRIS

difficult ★★★

The iris is an elaborate but beautiful model. The diagram comes without a stem, but you can adapt the tulip's stem to fit (see page 32). The iris has a lot of folding so it's best to use thin, smooth, double-sided origami paper in the colour of your choice; purple and yellow would work well.

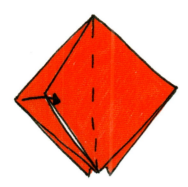

1 Start with the bird base, with the open end at the bottom

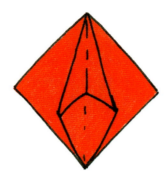

2 Lift the left-hand flap, put your finger inside and open it

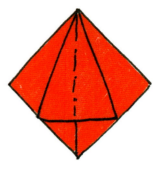

3 Press it down. Turn over the model and repeat.

4 Do the same with the two remaining flaps

5 Fold inwards on the dotted line, to the centre

6 Do the same on the right-hand side

7 Open the small flaps, then lift the flap underneath

8 Push up gently and press down to make a kite shape

9 Repeat steps 5 to 8 with the remaining three flaps

10 Fold down the small triangle on all four flaps

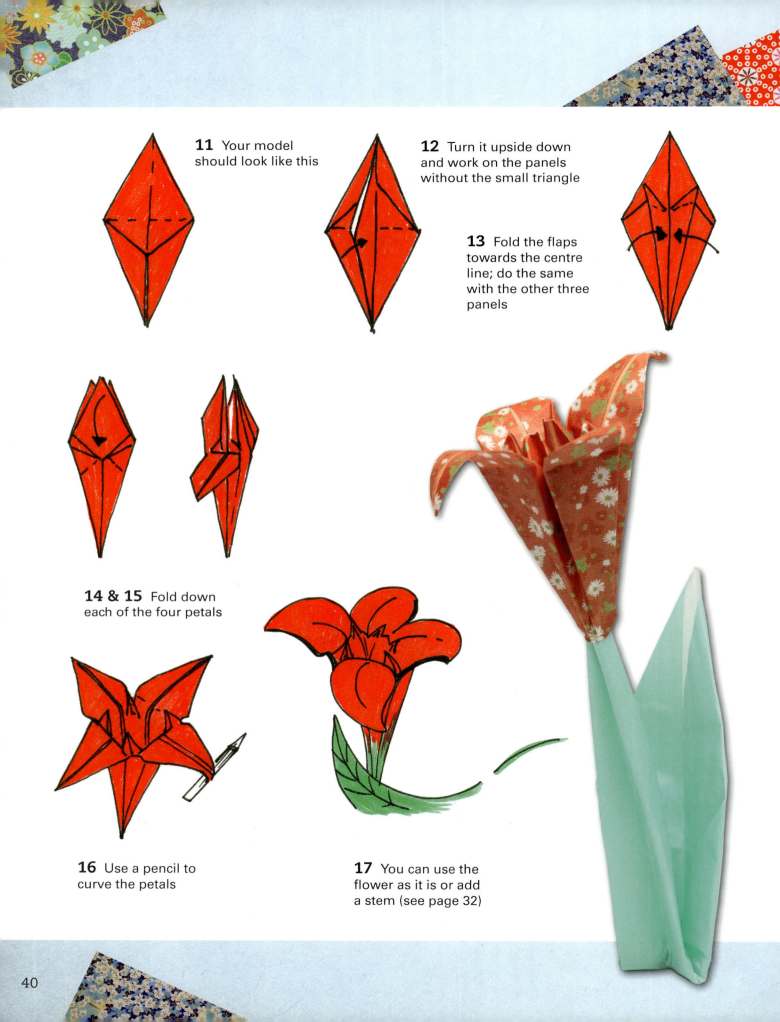

KUSUDAMA FLOWER

easy ★

This traditional Japanese origami model is easy to make, but care needs to be taken when assembling the five pieces at the end. It looks great using any type of origami paper and makes a lovely decoration.

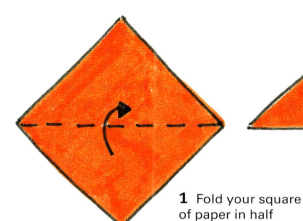

1 Fold your square of paper in half along the diagonal

2 Fold both corners to the centre

3 Crease along the dotted lines, as shown

4 Do the same on both sides

5 Put your finger in the outer pocket and make a squash fold

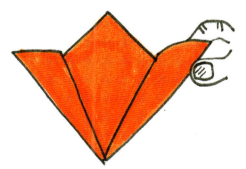

6 To make a squash fold, first open the pocket

7 Then squash it so that the side fold crease is down the centre of the pocket

41

8 Do this on both sides

9 Fold down the tips of the pockets

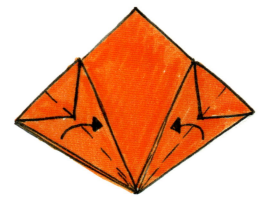
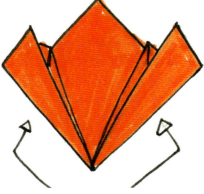

10 Now fold inwards along the dotted lines, as shown

11 Apply glue to the two surfaces indicated by the arrows, and press them together until dry

12 Place your finger in the finished petal to give it a curved shape

13 When you have done five petals, glue them together carefully, like this, to make the whole flower

MUSHROOM

medium ★★

This is a lovely, unusual model. It is best made with double-sided origami paper or patterned paper. It is not always easy to find a suitable pattern, so using coloured paper and adding spots and other decoration by hand works well.

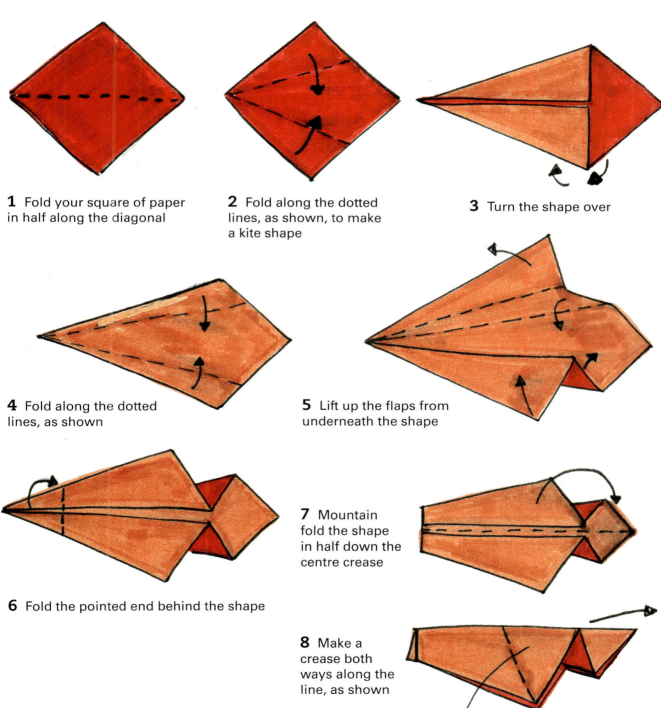

1 Fold your square of paper in half along the diagonal

2 Fold along the dotted lines, as shown, to make a kite shape

3 Turn the shape over

4 Fold along the dotted lines, as shown

5 Lift up the flaps from underneath the shape

6 Fold the pointed end behind the shape

7 Mountain fold the shape in half down the centre crease

8 Make a crease both ways along the line, as shown

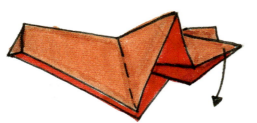

9 Inside reverse fold the point downwards so that it's inside the model

10 Make a crease, as shown

11 Fold the corners inside to create the mushroom 'cap' shape

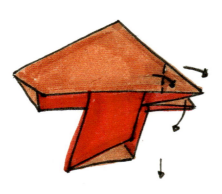

12 Fold the opposite corners inside

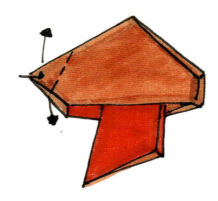

13 Inside reverse fold again on the other side, along the dotted line

14 Inside reverse fold the stalk along the crease, as shown

15 Decorate the model to make a mushroom of your choice

ROSE WITH LEAF

easy ★

This model is easy, but effective. It is best made using double-sided coloured paper for the rose and a simple green paper for the leaf. It works well used on cards or just as a decorative piece.

ROSE

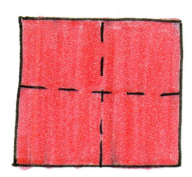

1 Using double-sided paper, place the sheet with the colour you want to show inside the rose face up. Fold in half, then in half again, and open it up.

2 Fold all the corners to the centre

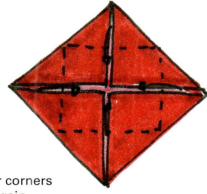

3 Fold all four corners to the centre again

4 Fold all four corners to the centre a third time

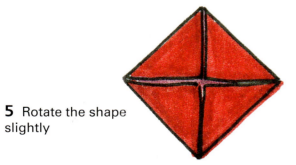

5 Rotate the shape slightly

6 Now fold the tips out along the dotted lines, as shown

45

7 Fold back the next layer of flaps

8 Fold back the last layer of flaps to reveal the inside colour

9 Mountain fold the tips on the base

LEAF

1 Fold the paper in half along the diagonal

2 Fold as shown to make a kite shape

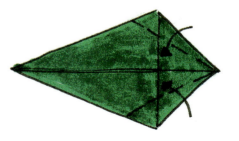

3 Fold again along the dotted lines

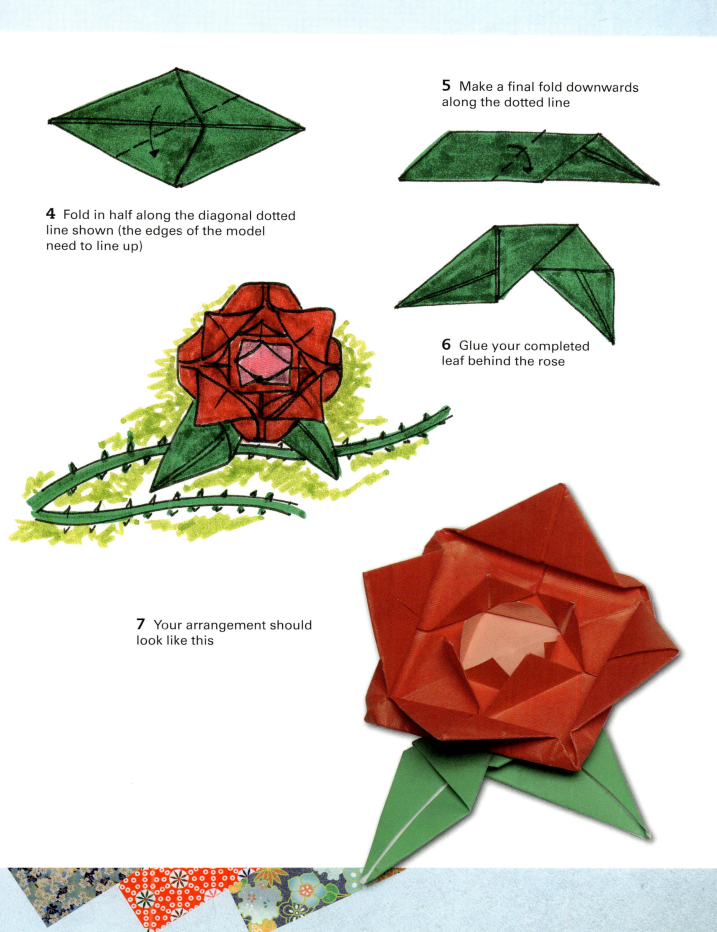

4 Fold in half along the diagonal dotted line shown (the edges of the model need to line up)

5 Make a final fold downwards along the dotted line

6 Glue your completed leaf behind the rose

7 Your arrangement should look like this

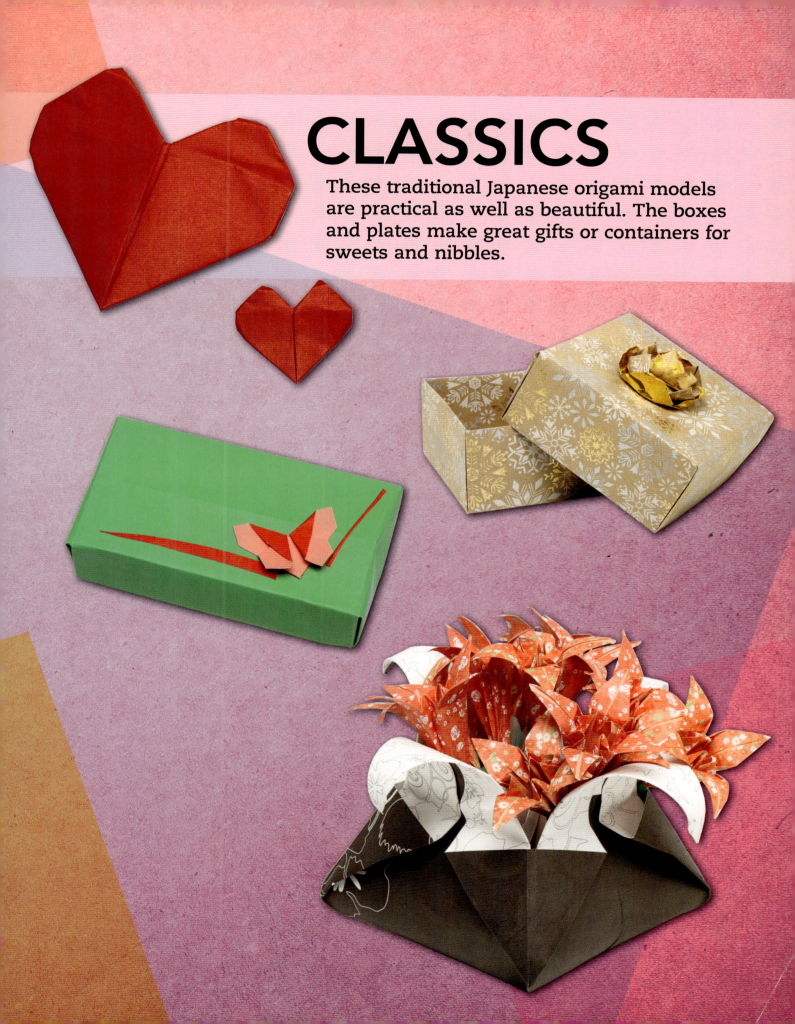

CLASSICS

These traditional Japanese origami models are practical as well as beautiful. The boxes and plates make great gifts or containers for sweets and nibbles.

MASU BOX

This is a traditional Japanese model. The initial folding is simple, but it becomes more difficult as you progress, following the creases made to close the shape as a box. This is why it is essential to create strong, clear creases. The box is made with two sheets of paper – one for the base and a slighter larger one for the lid. The paper has to be good quality and possibly thicker than normal origami paper. Patterned paper gives the best result.

1 Fold the paper in half

2 Fold in half again, then reopen it

3 Fold all four corners to the centre

4 Fold along the dotted lines to the centre

5 Make sure the flaps meet (but they shouldn't overlap)

6 Reopen and repeat the folding on the other two sides

7 Now open the side flaps completely. The square within the dotted lines will be the base of your box.

8 Open the side flaps, then pull up the two still-folded sides to make sides 1 and 2 of the box

9 Start folding in the left-hand flap towards the centre

medium ★★

 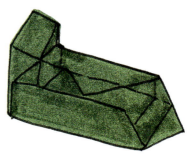

10 & 11 The paper should fold inwards on the creases to allow for this (see left and right)

12 Fold the flap over and tuck it into the base of the box to form side 3

13 Do the same with the other flap to create side 4

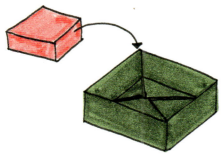

14 Once this part of the box is complete, make the lid by repeating the steps using a slightly larger square of paper. You can make a pretty decoration by pleat folding a small piece of paper into a fan shape.

RECTANGULAR BOX

This model is very similar to the masu box, but rectangular rather than square. The folding is different at the beginning, then it follows the same rules as the other box. Again, any type of origami paper can be used. I usually add decorations to the lids of both boxes, sometimes with traditional origami and other times with my own invented shapes.

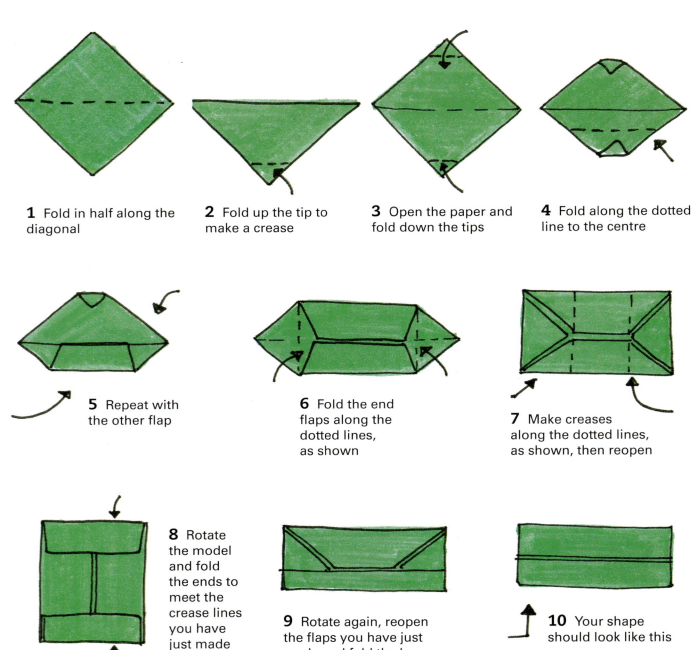

1 Fold in half along the diagonal

2 Fold up the tip to make a crease

3 Open the paper and fold down the tips

4 Fold along the dotted line to the centre

5 Repeat with the other flap

6 Fold the end flaps along the dotted lines, as shown

7 Make creases along the dotted lines, as shown, then reopen

8 Rotate the model and fold the ends to meet the crease lines you have just made

9 Rotate again, reopen the flaps you have just made and fold the long sides up to the centre line

10 Your shape should look like this

medium ★★

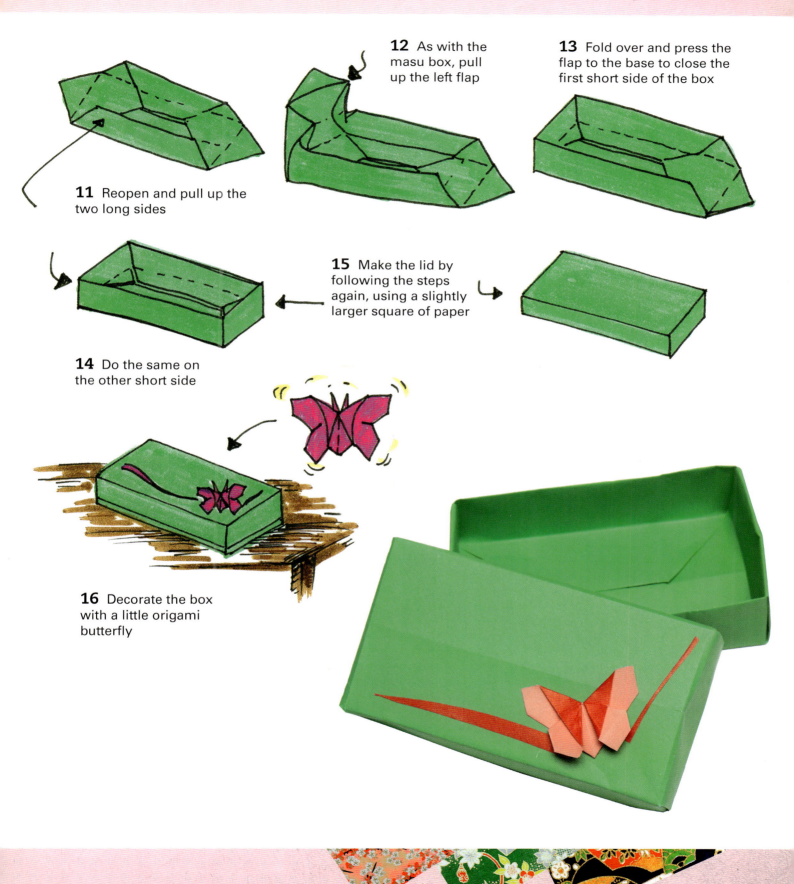

11 Reopen and pull up the two long sides

12 As with the masu box, pull up the left flap

13 Fold over and press the flap to the base to close the first short side of the box

14 Do the same on the other short side

15 Make the lid by following the steps again, using a slightly larger square of paper

16 Decorate the box with a little origami butterfly

SWEET CONTAINER

This modular container is easy to make, pretty and useful. It is created with five sheets of paper, which are then glued together. Any coloured origami paper will do for this. Sweet containers are used in Japan to give sweets as gifts, but you can use it for any small objects, such as jewellery or stationery.

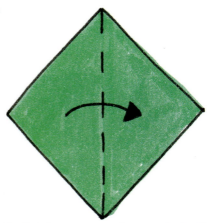

1 Fold a square of paper in half along the diagonal

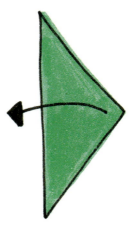

2 Reopen it

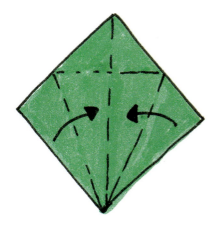

3 Fold it as shown to make a kite shape

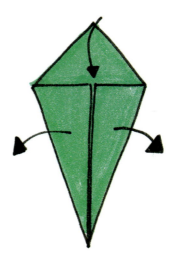

4 Reopen the long triangles and fold down the smaller triangle

5 Fold along the dotted line towards the centre

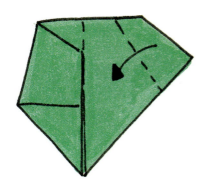

6 Repeat with the right-hand flap

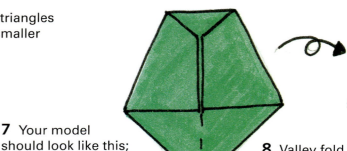

7 Your model should look like this; turn the shape over

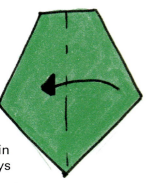

8 Valley fold in half lengthways

easy ★

9 Fold the point up along the crease line

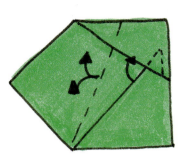

10 Tuck inside, as shown, and close the big flap

11 Fold down a small triangle on the top right-hand corner

12 Open the corner up again, then inside reverse fold the centre crease at the end

13 This shape gives you one segment of your container

14 Make four more identical segments and glue them together, as shown

STAR BOX

This traditional Japanese model can be used as a container or decorative piece. It is quite easy to make and looks particularly good made from patterned or double-sided paper.

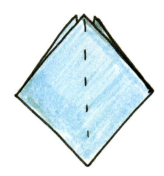

1 Start with a bird base, open at the top

2 Fold along the lines towards the centre

3 Turn over and repeat step 2

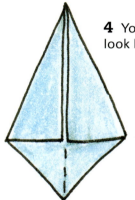

4 Your model should look like this

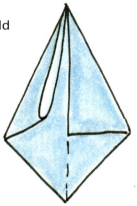

5 Open the left-hand flap

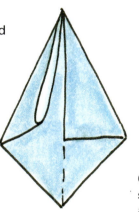

6 Press it down so that it makes a small kite

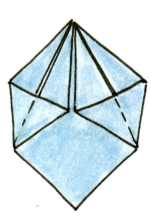

7 Do the same with the right-hand flap

8 Turn the model over and repeat steps 6 and 7

9 Fold the outer half of each flap under the other half

easy ⭐

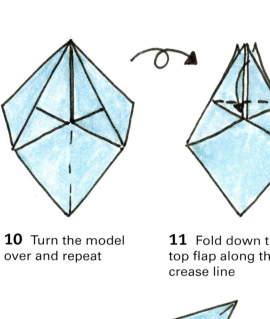

10 Turn the model over and repeat

11 Fold down the top flap along the crease line

12 Repeat with the other three flaps

13 Pull out the flaps and shape the box with your fingers

14 The final piece should look like this

57

TEA PLATE

This elegant and decorative plate is used in Japan for offering sweets with tea. It is slightly more advanced and should be made with thin paper or proper origami paper. It is usually made with patterned paper.

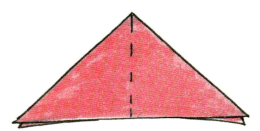

1 Start with a water-bomb base

2 Fold the flaps up along the crease line

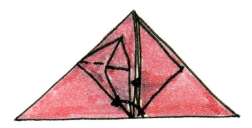

3 Open the left-hand flap

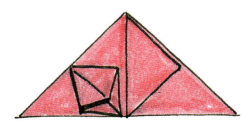

4 Press it down (the shape makes a small square)

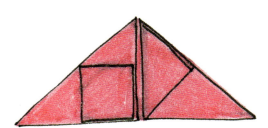

5 Do the same with the right-hand flap

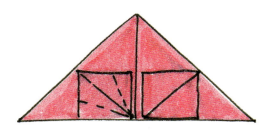

6 Fold on the dotted lines to make a mini-kite shape

7 Repeat with the right-hand flap

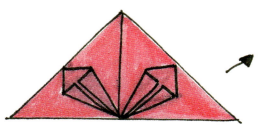 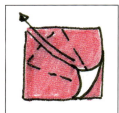

8 Make a horizontal crease at the top of the kite shapes, then open up the flaps and flatten them

medium ★★

9 Your model should look like this

10 Fold the kite shapes towards the centre to make them sit closer together

11 & 12 Now repeat steps 2–9 with the two flaps behind the shapes you have made

13 Your finished tea plate can be filled with little sweets

HEART

The heart is a traditional model best made with thin paper because of the many overlapping folds. It's important to mould it at the end to make it more curved, as a heart should be. The finished piece may look a bit rigid, so it's worth pressing and shaping the angles carefully. This heart can be given to a loved one to use as a bookmark.

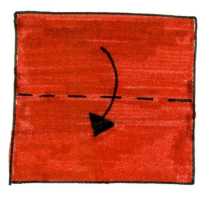

1 Fold the paper in half horizontally

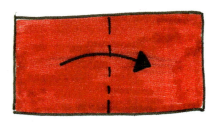

2 Fold in half again

3 Reopen the small square

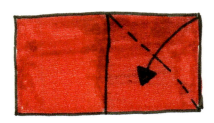

4 Fold down along the dotted line, as shown

5 Do the same on the left-hand side

6 Turn the shape over

7 Rotate so that it is upside down

8 Fold in along the crease lines shown

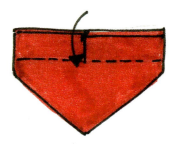

9 Fold down the top flap along the dotted lines

medium ★★

10 Open up the top flaps on both sides

11 Press down the corners to flatten the shape

12 Fold the two small top flaps along the lines shown

13 Your model should look like this

14 Turn the shape over and complete the modelling with your hands

15 The final piece will look like this

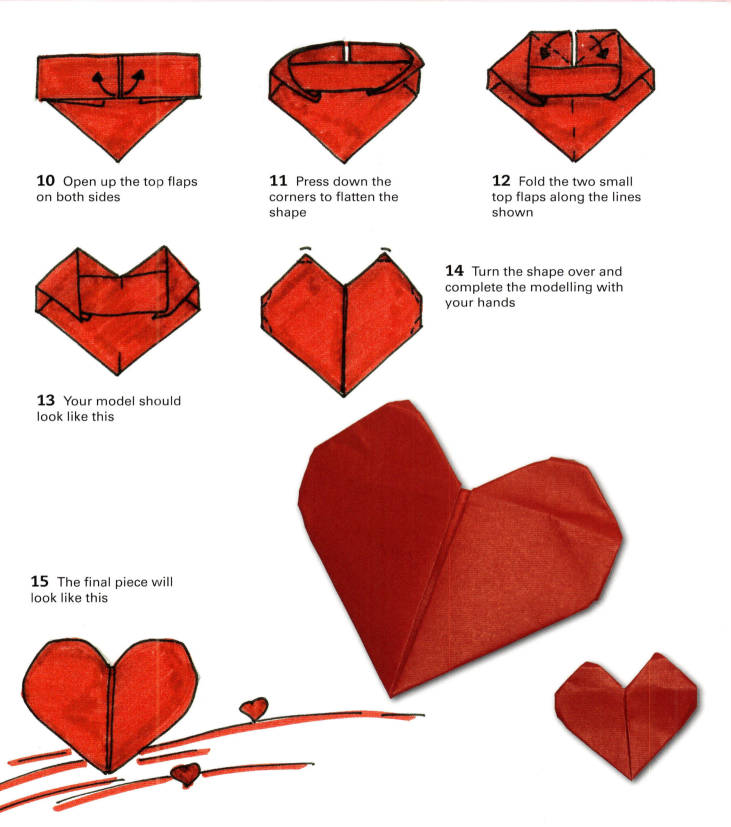

61

A SIMPLE BAG

This model is delightful yet very easy to make; it can be created in various sizes and used as a gift bag. Only a little folding is required and decoration can be added to make it more appealing. You can use ordinary origami coloured or patterned paper, but for very large sizes it may be advisable to use thicker paper or card.

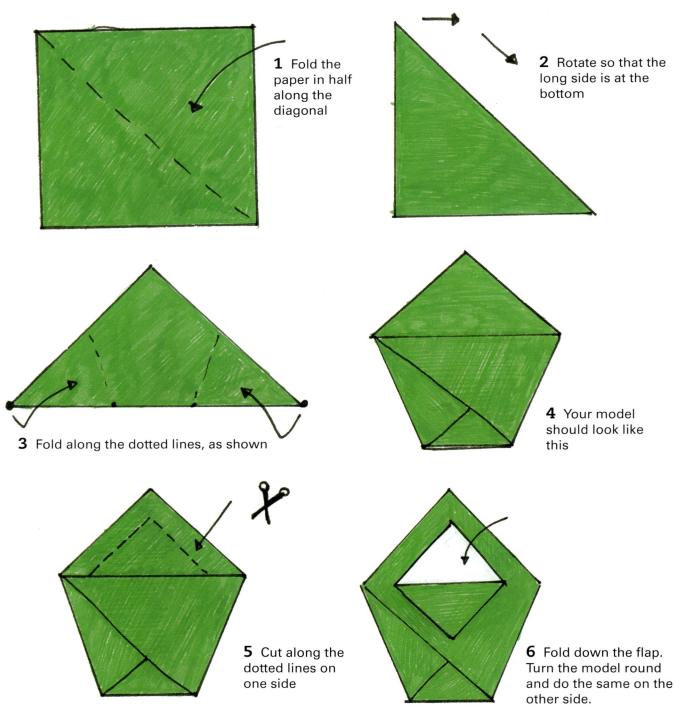

1 Fold the paper in half along the diagonal

2 Rotate so that the long side is at the bottom

3 Fold along the dotted lines, as shown

4 Your model should look like this

5 Cut along the dotted lines on one side

6 Fold down the flap. Turn the model round and do the same on the other side.

easy ⭐

7 You can decorate the flaps however you like – a small origami fish or flower looks good!

63

GEISHA CARD

This model is slightly different from the other origami in this book. You will need two sheets of paper, one for the body and one for the sleeves. For best results, use double-sided paper. You can be flexible with decoration, patterns and accessories for the geisha and for the kimono.

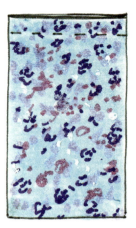 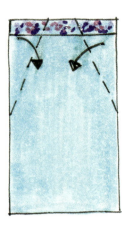 

1 Using a piece of rectangular origami paper with the patterned side facing upwards, fold down the top along the dotted line

2 Turn the paper over and fold along the dotted lines, as shown. This will give you the top of the kimono.

3 Fold in the right-hand side along the vertical dotted line

4 Fold the right-hand flap back along the dotted line, as shown

5 Fold in the left-hand side along the vertical dotted line

6 Fold this flap back along the dotted line, as shown

medium ★★

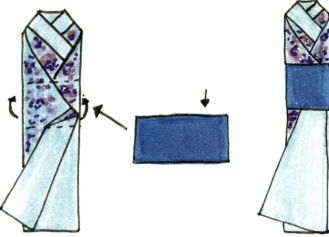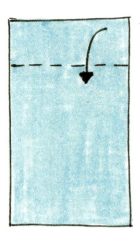

7 Cut a strip of contrasting paper and wrap it round the middle of the model to make the belt ('obi'). Glue in place at the back.

8 This completes the body of the geisha

9 To make the sleeves, take a rectangle of paper and place it with the patterned side down. Fold down along the dotted line.

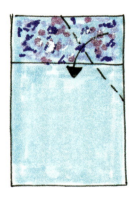

10 Fold in along the dotted line, as shown

11 Fold up along the dotted line

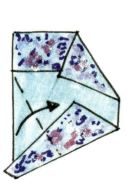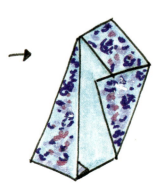

12 Fold in again, overlapping the paper

13 Rotate, as shown

14 With the sleeves in this position, glue them to the back of the geisha model

15 The completed model will look like this

65

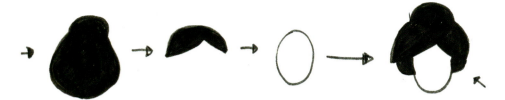

16 To make the geisha's head, cut two shapes from black paper (for the hair) and an oval from white paper (for the face). Glue the pieces together, as shown. The decoration for the hair is an oval of coloured paper folded in half (see right).

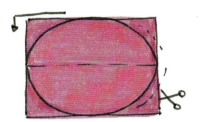

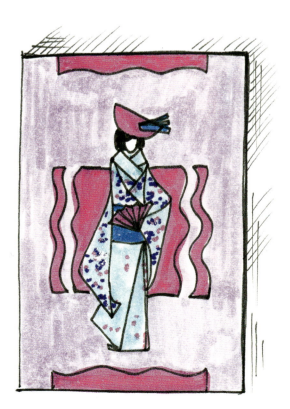

17 You can make a fan by pleat folding a small square of paper and pinching it together at one end

18 You can either glue your geisha onto a card or use her as a bookmark

CHAIR

This is my own design, based on a study of several different chair models. It is important to fold carefully and maintain the correct proportions so that the chair stands properly. You can make it any size and use it as a decoration or to place something light on. Try experimenting and expanding on this model with various types of paper, card or other materials.

1 Fold a square of paper in half, then in half again.

2 Open it up and fold each corner to the centre

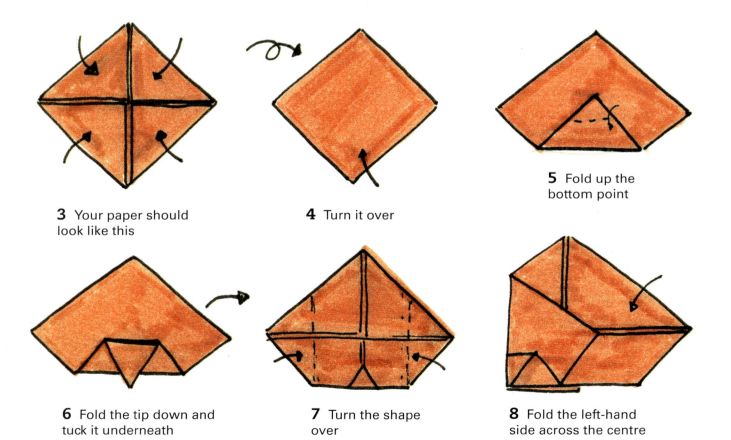

3 Your paper should look like this

4 Turn it over

5 Fold up the bottom point

6 Fold the tip down and tuck it underneath

7 Turn the shape over

8 Fold the left-hand side across the centre

medium ★★

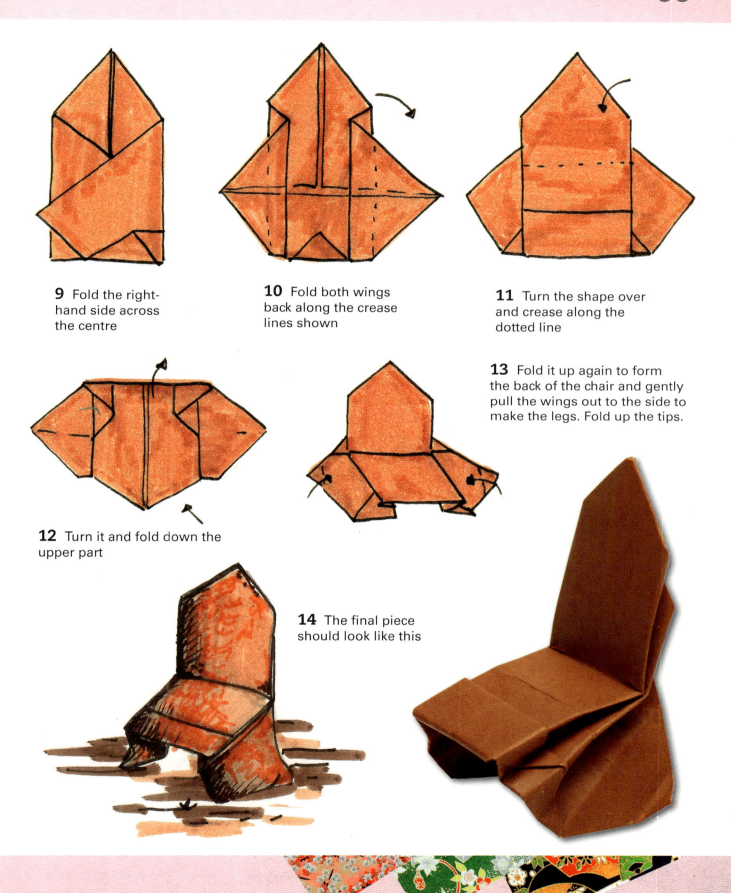

9 Fold the right-hand side across the centre

10 Fold both wings back along the crease lines shown

11 Turn the shape over and crease along the dotted line

12 Turn it and fold down the upper part

13 Fold it up again to form the back of the chair and gently pull the wings out to the side to make the legs. Fold up the tips.

14 The final piece should look like this

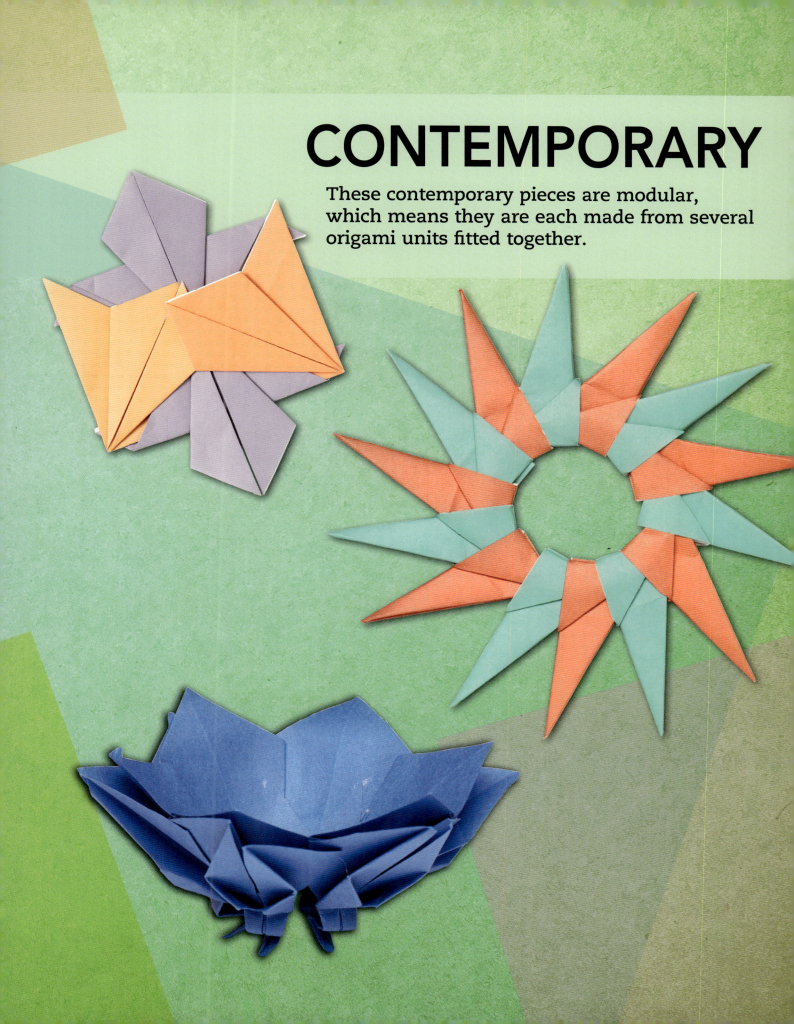
CONTEMPORARY

These contemporary pieces are modular, which means they are each made from several origami units fitted together.

COASTER

Modular origami is created by assembling repeated shapes. These designs tend to be abstract, but sometimes resemble real objects and can be used for decoration and even as containers. It is interesting to try different forms before gluing them together; that way you can test out the possibilities for your model. This contemporary origami style is open to interpretation and leaves you free to use your imagination when making your model.

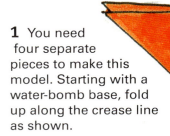

1 You need four separate pieces to make this model. Starting with a water-bomb base, fold up along the crease line as shown.

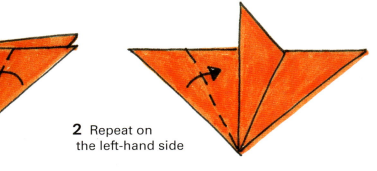

2 Repeat on the left-hand side

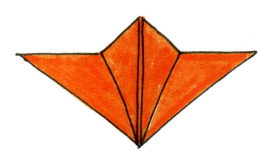

3 Your shape should look like this. Put it to one side while you make another three exactly the same.

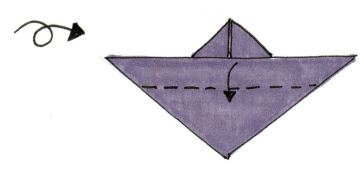

4 Taking two of the shapes you have made, continue as follows. Turn the model over and fold down along the line.

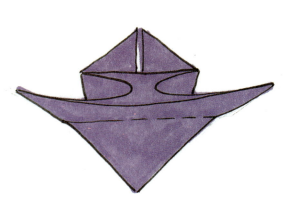

5 Press down, flattening the small flaps in the middle

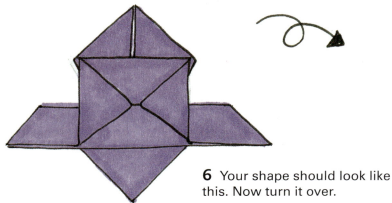

6 Your shape should look like this. Now turn it over.

medium ★★

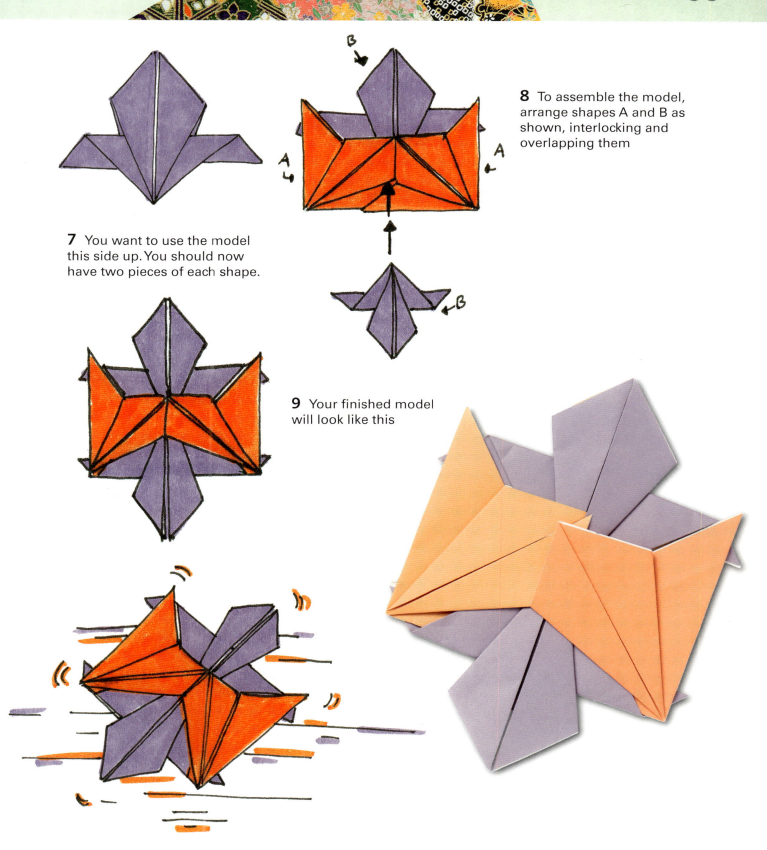

7 You want to use the model this side up. You should now have two pieces of each shape.

8 To assemble the model, arrange shapes A and B as shown, interlocking and overlapping them

9 Your finished model will look like this

BOWL

This is a new model I have created, again using repeated origami for the design. The bowl looks nice as a nest for little Easter eggs. It's best to use double-sided origami for this model.

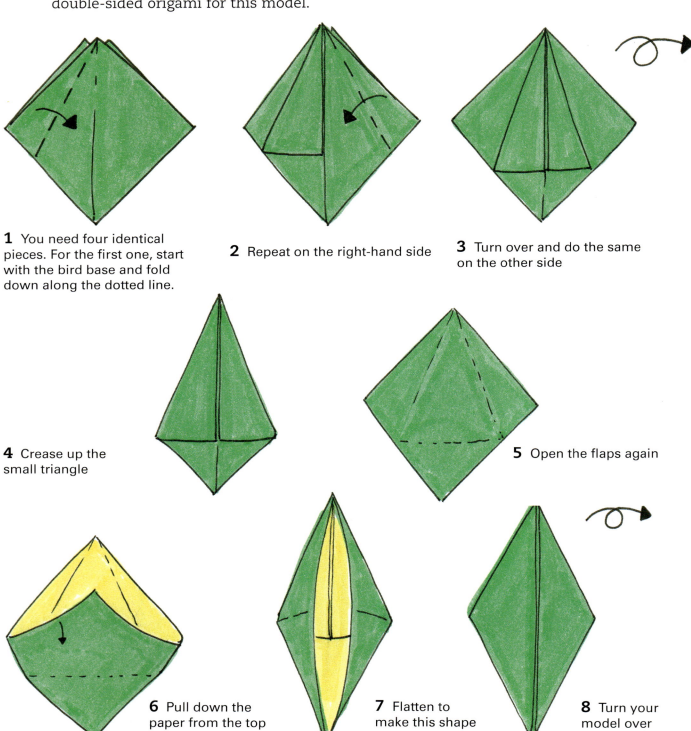

1 You need four identical pieces. For the first one, start with the bird base and fold down along the dotted line.

2 Repeat on the right-hand side

3 Turn over and do the same on the other side

4 Crease up the small triangle

5 Open the flaps again

6 Pull down the paper from the top

7 Flatten to make this shape

8 Turn your model over

medium ★★

9 Open the left-hand top flap and press it down to look like a small kite

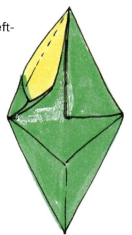

10 Do the same with the right-hand top flap

11 Fold down along the dotted line, as shown

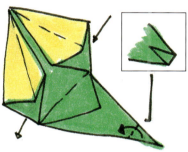

12 This shape makes one of your four pieces. Fold up the tip along the dotted line.

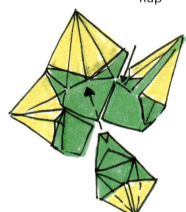

13 When you have made four pieces exactly the same, glue the folded-up tips together

14 Your finished bowl will look like this

75

SPIKY STAR

This is the only model in the contemporary section that I didn't invent myself. It is a simple but lovely and eye-catching spiky star, perfect to use as a door hanging at Christmas. It's easily made with 14 sheets of paper of various colours, which are then assembled to make the star shape. Each piece has a small pocket, so you can tuck them into one another, but I'd recommend gluing them together as well. You can use sparkly paper to give the star a festive feel, but any type of origami paper will do.

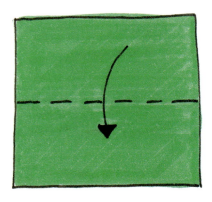

1 Mountain fold your square of paper in half and then unfold it

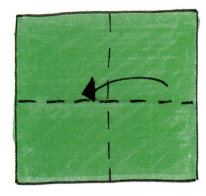

2 Fold and unfold again, as shown

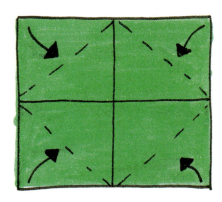

3 Fold all corners to the centre

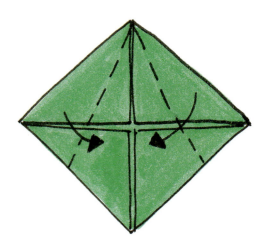

4 Fold along the dotted lines to make a kite shape

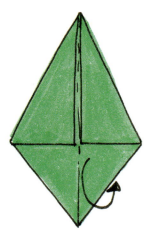

5 Fold the bottom triangle behind

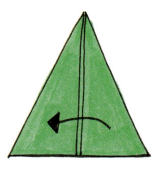

6 Fold the shape in half to close

easy ★

7 Your finished piece should look like this

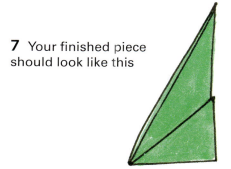

8 Make 13 more pieces in exactly the same way and assemble the model by tucking the pointed corners of one piece inside the flaps of the next

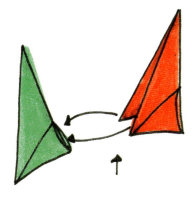

9 Your assembled star will look like this

STANDING PLATE

This is a new model of mine. It is quite easy to make, but the assembly is a little more difficult. You need six identical pieces. The plate is very decorative and can be made with normal origami paper, but if you use stronger, larger sheets of paper it can hold sweets, chocolates or small objects, or even be used as a centrepiece.

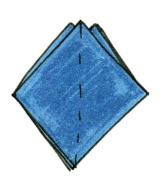

1 Start with the bird base, open end at the top

2 Fold along the dotted lines as shown, then unfold

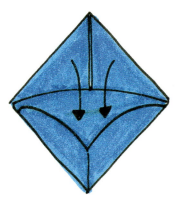

3 Pull down the top piece of paper

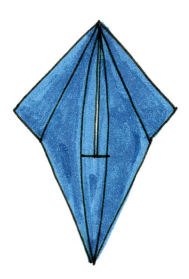

4 Press down and flatten it

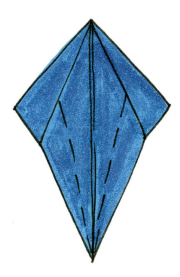

5 Fold inwards along the dotted lines

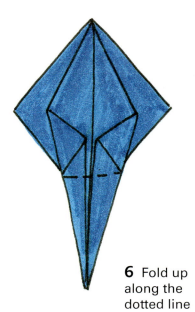

6 Fold up along the dotted line

medium ★★

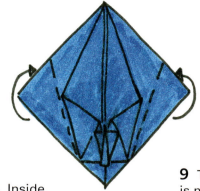
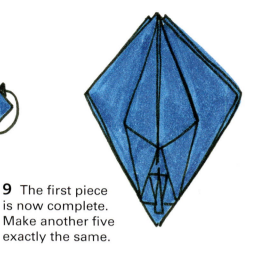

7 Fold down along the lower line and then up along line the higher one

8 Inside reverse fold the sides so that they are inside the piece

9 The first piece is now complete. Make another five exactly the same.

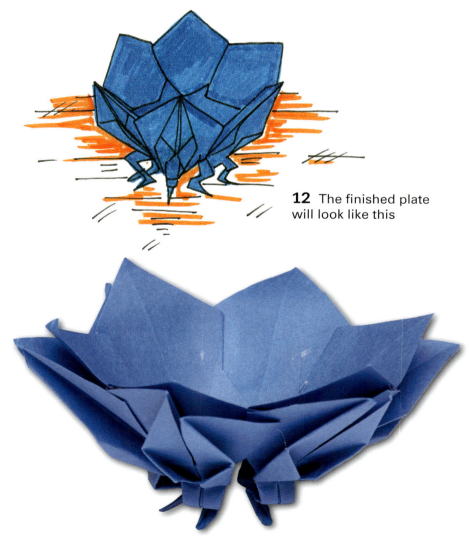

10 Glue the pieces together (see diagram)

11 Cut out a small piece of paper and glue it inside to complete the base of the plate

12 The finished plate will look like this

HUMMINGBIRD

This model is my personal version of a bird, created with two pieces of paper. The first is the body where the folding is a bit elaborate and second is the wings, which are very easy to make. I usually glue the pieces together. This elegant model can be used as a decoration for events or for gift boxes. Use traditional coloured origami paper for this.

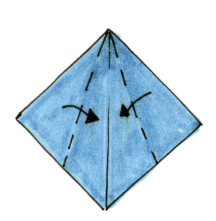 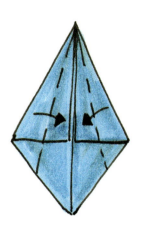 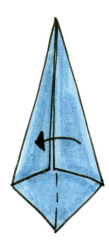 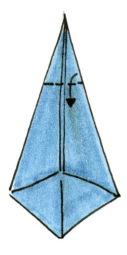

1 Fold your square of paper along the lines towards the centre to make a kite shape

2 Fold to the centre again along the dotted lines

3 Fold in half to crease, then unfold

4 Fold down the tip along the dotted line

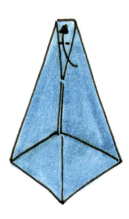 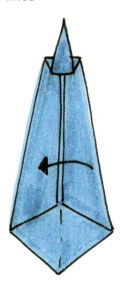  

5 Fold up along the dotted line

6 Fold the model in half again

7 For the head and neck, make a crease and push the tip in so that it is at right angles

8 Crease along the dotted line and reverse fold, pushing the neck in again

difficult ★★★

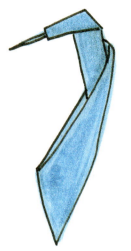

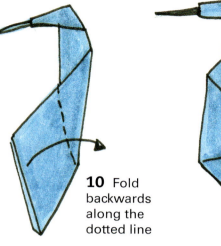

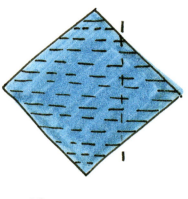

9 Your shape should look like this

10 Fold backwards along the dotted line

11 The body is now complete

12 For the wings, pleat fold the other sheet of paper, like an accordion

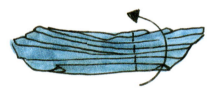

13 Fold upwards along the dotted line

14 Open the wings and fix them to the body with glue or double-sided tape

15 The finished hummingbird looks like this

81

CONTEMPORARY FORM

This is another new, eye-catching model with an interesting geometric shape. It is easy to make, but a little tricky to assemble. It can be created with any type of reasonably thin coloured paper.

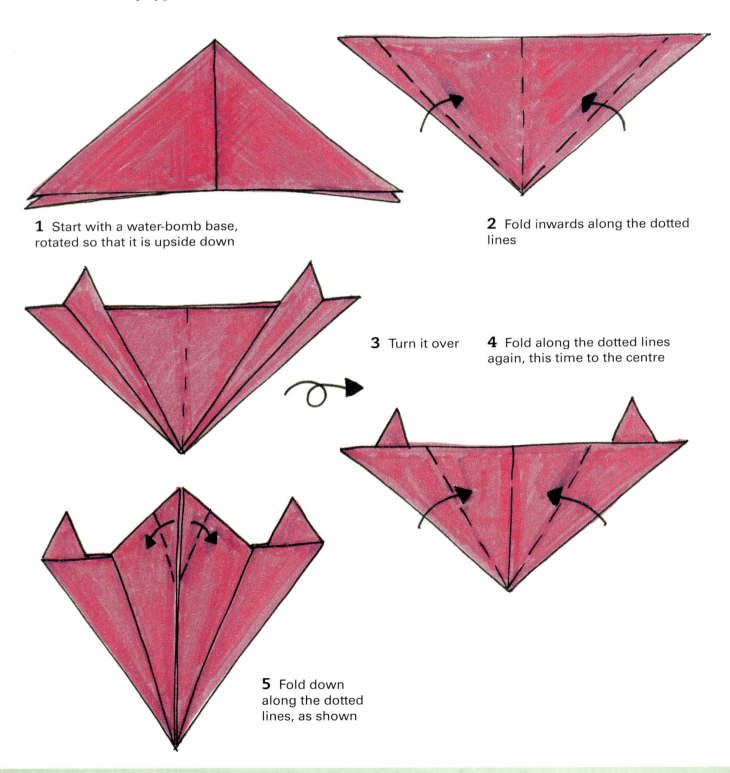

1 Start with a water-bomb base, rotated so that it is upside down

2 Fold inwards along the dotted lines

3 Turn it over

4 Fold along the dotted lines again, this time to the centre

5 Fold down along the dotted lines, as shown

medium ✪✪

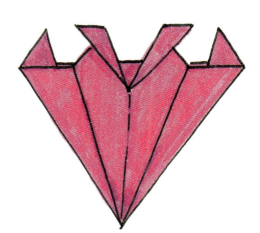

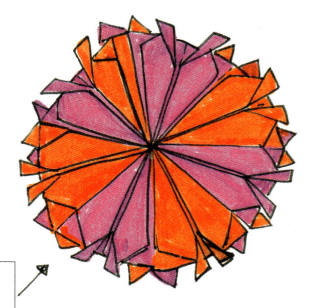

6 Your first piece is complete – you need seven of these to make the model

7 Glue each piece behind the central flaps and attach to the wing of the next one to create an interlocking shape

83

KIRIGAMI

While origami involves paper folding, with kirigami you fold and cut the paper to make pretty decorative pieces.

FANTASY TREE

easy ★

The word 'kirigami' translates as 'cutting paper' (the verb 'kiri' meaning 'to cut'). Kirigami is a traditional pastime in Japan, but it is also becoming popular in Western countries. It's generally important to use paper that is neither too thick nor too thin. Thin paper will make the design unstable and thick paper will be difficult to cut when folded. As with origami, there is some basic folding and a range of bases. The main bases are square, rectangle and triangle, with variations in terms of the number of times the paper is folded. It's worth using double-sided paper for all the models.

This first design is very easy to make. I created it because I am fascinated by fairies and fantasy themes.

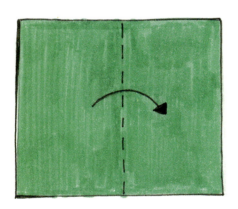

1 Fold a square of paper in half from left to right. As the paper is only folded in half for this model, thicker paper or card can be used.

2 Draw your tree design in pencil

3 Cut around the shape

4 Open the paper to see your completed tree

5 The shape can stand on a table and be used for 3D designs and scenes

TURTLES DECORATION

medium ★★

You can make the frame for this piece either straight or wavy. I made mine wavy because I was inspired by sea turtles and the importance of the turtle symbol in Japan. You can use any paper, but it shouldn't be too thick.

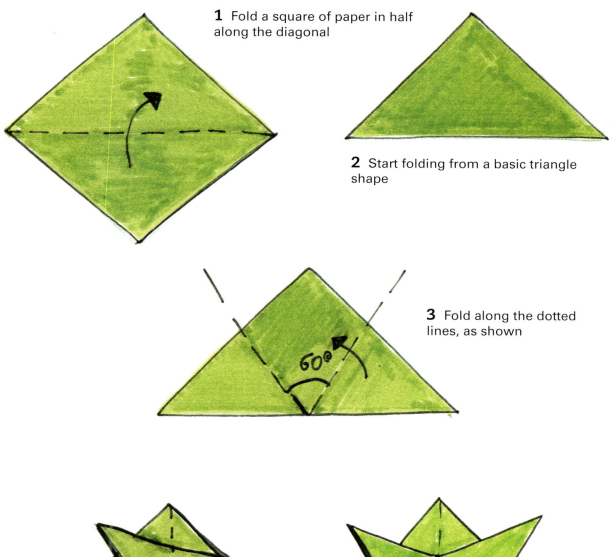

1 Fold a square of paper in half along the diagonal

2 Start folding from a basic triangle shape

3 Fold along the dotted lines, as shown

4 Fold the right-hand side in, as shown

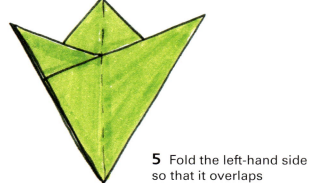

5 Fold the left-hand side so that it overlaps

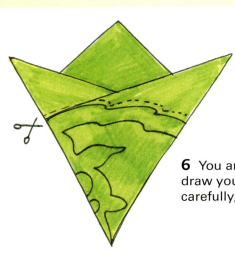

6 You are now ready to draw your turtle outline carefully, as shown

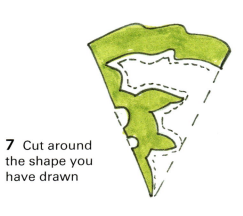

7 Cut around the shape you have drawn

8 When opened out, your finished piece should look like this

BIRDS

medium ★★

For this design, I took inspiration from various books and styles of cutting as well as my passion for birds. It requires careful cutting. As the paper is folded a few times, it is advisable to use normal origami paper; don't use card, as this will make it impossible to cut.

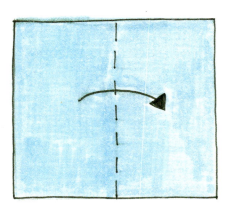

1 Start with a rectangle base. Fold it in half from left to right.

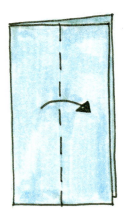

2 Fold in half again from left to right

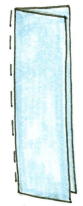

3 The shape is now ready for drawing

4 In pencil, draw your birds onto the model, making sure that your drawing touches both sides of the paper

5 Carefully cut around the shape

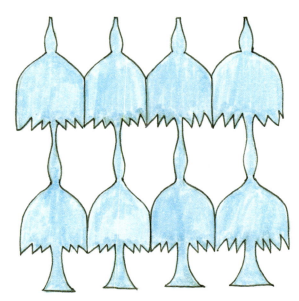

6 When opened out, your final piece should look like this

CURVY DECORATION

This design is easy but eye-catching and can be used as an elegant home decoration. For this project, I took inspiration from floral Art Deco designs. The best medium to use is thin card in any colour, or heavy, patterned paper.

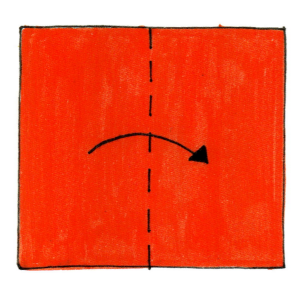

1 Fold your square of paper in half from left to right

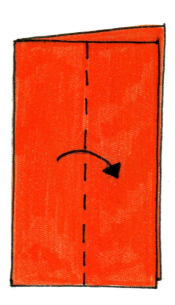

2 Fold in half again from left to right

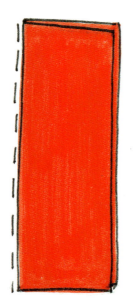

3 The shape is now ready for drawing

4 In pencil, draw your design onto the paper, making sure that your drawing touches both sides of the paper

easy ★

5 Carefully cut around the shape

6 Open out the paper

7 Your final piece should look like this

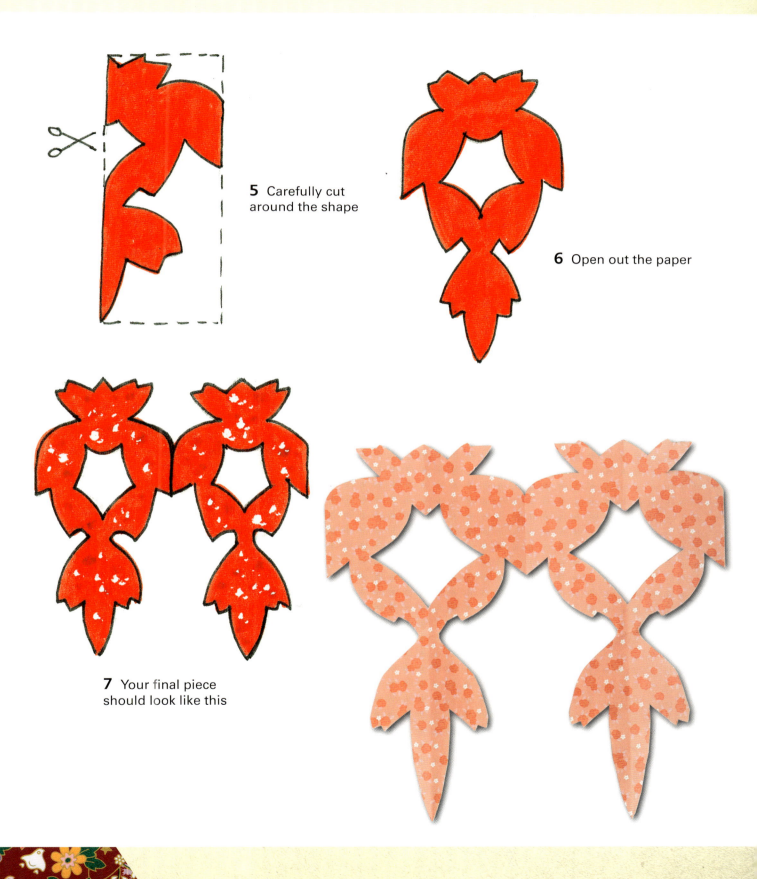

91

CHERRY BLOSSOM

This model is slightly different from other kirigami because it is created by cutting only part of the shapes to produce a design in relief. You can create any shape you like, but it is advisable to keep it simple if you are a beginner. You can use origami paper, but it works best with thicker paper; double-sided gives a great effect.

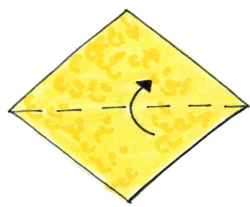

1 Start with a triangle base. Fold your square of paper in half along the diagonal.

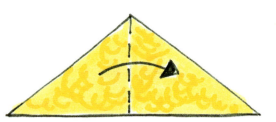

2 Fold the triangle shape in half along the dotted line

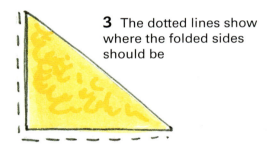

3 The dotted lines show where the folded sides should be

4 Draw two flowers along the folded sides, then cut them out, stopping just before the base of the left-hand shape and the left-hand edge of the bottom shape (see arrows)

5 When you open the paper, one petal of each flower will be attached, as shown

medium ★★

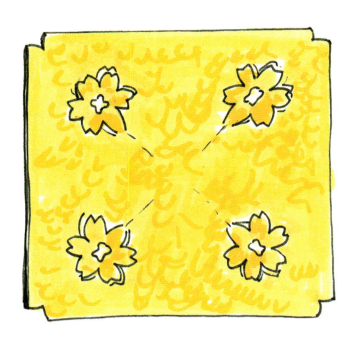

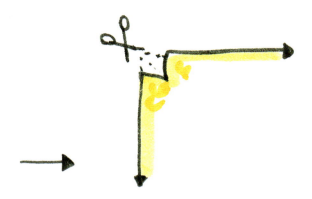

6 Your final piece will look like this

7 You can make small cuts at each corner to make it more decorative

TABLE CENTREPIECE

This idea comes from the mandala, the circle symbol of the universe. It is quite simple to make, but attention is needed when folding the base and it is best to use thin paper rather than thick card.

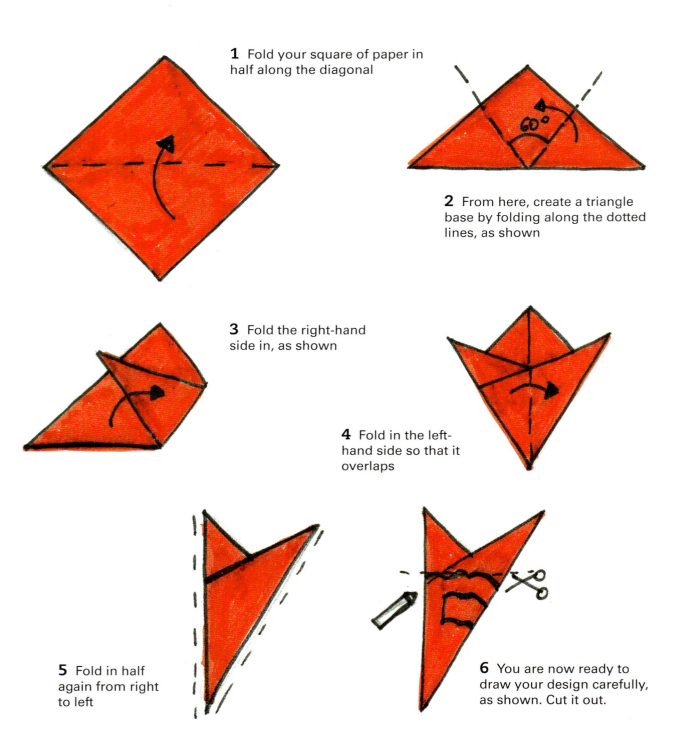

1 Fold your square of paper in half along the diagonal

2 From here, create a triangle base by folding along the dotted lines, as shown

3 Fold the right-hand side in, as shown

4 Fold in the left-hand side so that it overlaps

5 Fold in half again from right to left

6 You are now ready to draw your design carefully, as shown. Cut it out.

medium ★★

7 Open up the paper

8 Your final piece should look like this

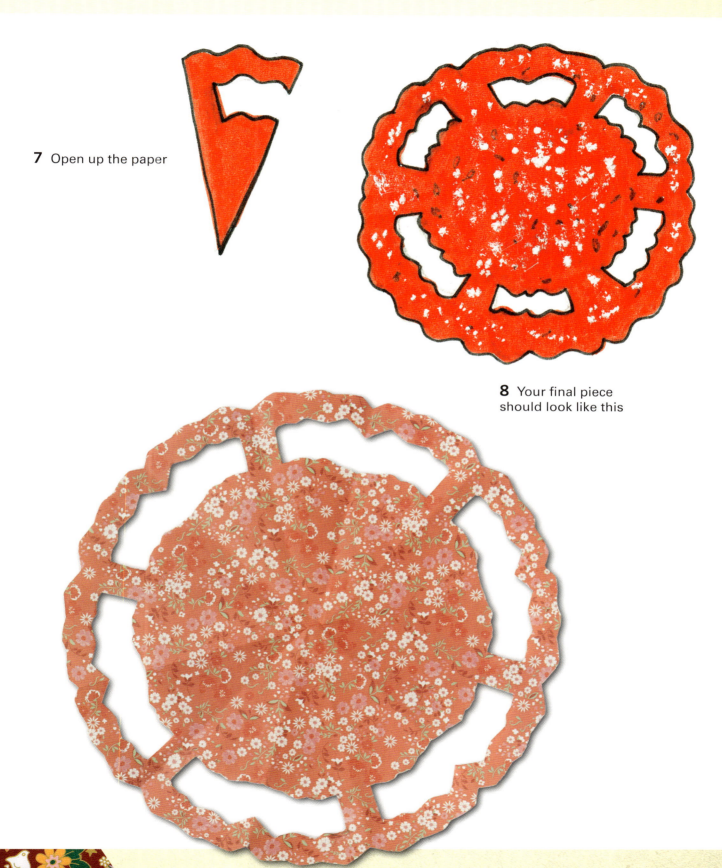

Stockists

The following suppliers stock a wide range of materials for origami enthusiasts:

www.aliexpress.com/w/wholesale-origami-paper.html

www.foldedsquare.com

www.japancentre.com/en/categories/1057-origami

www.origami.com.au

www.origami-fun.com

www.origamipapermonster.com

www.theorigamipapershop.com

www.origamishop.us

www.paperchase.co.uk

www.roze.co.uk/origami-paper-22-c.asp

supplies.britishorigami.info

www.thejapaneseshop.co.uk

All illustrations and models by Monika Cilmi